BFI FILM CLASSICS

· ·

Rob White
SERIES EDITOR

Edward Buscombe, Colin MacCabe, David Meeker and Markku Salmi
SERIES CONSULTANTS

Launched in 1992, BFI Film Classics is a series of books that introduces, interprets and honours 360 landmark works of world cinema. The series includes a wide range of approaches and critical styles, reflecting the diverse ways we appreciate, analyse and enjoy great films.

A treasury that keeps on delivering ... any film person needs the whole collection.
Independent on Sunday

Magnificently concentrated examples of flowing freeform critical poetry.
Uncut

A formidable body of work collectively generating some fascinating insights into the evolution of cinema.
Times Higher Education Supplement

The definitive film companion essays.
Hotdog

The choice of authors is as judicious, eclectic and original as the choice of titles.
Positif

Estimable.
Boston Globe

Invaluable.
Los Angeles Times

T0347045

The series is a landmark in the history of film criticism.
Quarterly Review of Film and Video

Well written, impeccably researched and beautifully presented ... as a publishing venture, it is difficult to fault.
Film Ireland

Carol Reed (centre-left) in Vienna, autumn 1948

THE THIRD MAN

Rob White

THE BRITISH FILM INSTITUTE
Bloomsbury Publishing Plc
50 Bedford Square, London, WC1B 3DP, UK
1385 Broadway, New York, NY 10018, USA
29 Earlsfort Terrace, Dublin 2, Ireland

BLOOMSBURY is a trademark of Bloomsbury Publishing Plc

First published by the British Film Institute in 2003
Reprinted by Palgrave in 2011
Reprinted by Bloomsbury in 2018 (twice), 2019, 2020, 2022, 2023, 2025
on behalf of the
British Film Institute
21 Stephen Street, London W1T 1LN
www.bfi.org.uk

The BFI is the lead organisation for film in the UK and the distributor of Lottery funds
for film. Our mission is to ensure that film is central to our cultural life, in particular by
supporting and nurturing the next generation of filmmakers and audiences. We serve a
public role which covers the cultural, creative and economic aspects of film in the UK.

Series design by Andrew Barron & Collis Clements Associates

ISBN: PB: 978-0-8517-0963-5

Series: BFI Film Classics

Typeset by D R Bungay Associates, Burghfield, Berkshire
Printed and bound in Great Britain

To find out more about our authors and books visit www.bloomsbury.com
and sign up for our newsletters.

CONTENTS

. . . .

Acknowledgments *6*

'The Third Man' *7*

Notes *81*

Credits *84*

Select Bibliography *86*

ACKNOWLEDGMENTS

Personal thanks to Rich Brown, Tom Cabot, Nick Holland, Ed Lawrenson, Laura Mulvey, Sarah Prosser, Antonia Quirke, A. L. Rees and Heather Stewart.

Many colleagues at the British Film Institute were generous with their support or assistance. Richard Paterson enabled crucial research leave. Mark Duguid commissioned work on Carol Reed and *The Third Man* for screenonline.org.uk. Fleur Buckley, Kathleen Dickson, Bryony Dixon and Steve Tollervey arranged access to material in the National Film and Television Archive. Janet Moat and Claire Thomas were courteous custodians of the Special Collections of paper material. Sean Delaney, David Sharp and many of their colleagues made the Library a pleasure to use. The staff of the Stills, Posters and Designs section were equally hospitable. Tony Mechele loaned tapes of *The Third Man* TV series. Ronnie Hackston dug up some New Romantic memorabilia.

Farther afield, Roger Hebblethwaite provided a bibliography of Austrian history. Jim Mather supplied some fascinating contemporary photographs of occupied Vienna. Erika Toal and Caren Willig kindly advised on points of translation and transcription.

S. S. Prawer shared his insight into European culture in general, and *The Third Man* in particular, in a most rewarding correspondence.

Sincere thanks to all the above-named.

Dudley Andrew, Nick James and Andrew Lockett read the manuscript and made comments that were greatly valued. David Meeker and Markku Salmi did so too, but that is as it should have been – this book would not have been written without their example, inspiration and conversation over a number of years.

Any errors of fact and judgment that remain – not to mention the curious flights of fancy – are the responsibility of no one other than the author.

'THE THIRD MAN'

. . . .

> There is no sun without shadow and it is necessary to know the night.
> Albert Camus, *The Myth of Sisyphus* (1942)

'I never knew the old Vienna before the war, with its Strauss music, its glamour and easy charm.'[1] The voice is English, the delivery laconic and brisk, the mood cosmopolitan but hard-bitten. 'Constantinople suited me better.' It is Carol Reed delivering the voiceover that sets the scene for *The Third Man*: 'I really got to know it in the classic period of the Black Market – we'd run anything, if people wanted it enough and had the money to pay. Of course, a situation like that does tempt amateurs – but you know they can't stay the course like a professional.'

The talk is of a new Vienna, after the war: an occupied city patrolled by soldiers from America, Britain, France and the Soviet Union, and a city partly in ruins, though, as the voice points out, 'it doesn't look any worse than a lot of other European cities – bombed about a bit'. There is, to listen to it, no lamentation here, nor any solemn reflection on the recent carnage – just unsentimental plain-speaking, clipped and fast.

But the shots in the mock-documentary opening sequence tell a slightly different story. There are racketeers selling boots, stockings and wristwatches. Deprivation shows in their stubbled faces. The body of an 'amateur' floats among hunks of cracked ice in grimy-looking water, the low sun glinting, the wreck of a ship partly visible at the left edge of the screen. These images, and the ones of structures reduced to rubble, sit uneasily with the shots showing an official world of order: Vienna's classical façades and statues, occupying troops on patrol or

Vienna after the war

parade. The damage done in war is evident in the sequence even though Reed's voiceover and the fast cutting (twenty-eight different shots in sixty-six seconds) discourage the viewer from dwelling on it.

And there is the music, played on a zither over the opening credits. It is also ambiguous. Like the montage of post-war Vienna it goes at a jaunty pace but there are darker things underneath its good cheer. It is music for bourgeois leisure, but something else can be heard in it too – unease, tension, some middle-European density.

It might not have been as fluent as this. Graham Greene, who wrote the screenplay, imagined, to begin with, a scene at Frankfurt airport where the protagonist Holly Martins is mistaken for an eminent man of letters. And David O. Selznick, who put up much of the money for the production, persisted in demanding more explanation of the protocol and administrative practicalities of four-power occupation. So presumably it was Reed's work to make the opening so quick and condensed. That would make sense. Reed was a pragmatic film-maker, ready to change style if necessary in order to keep things moving – a bit of a magpie, but one with clear goals in sight.

Selznick, though, undid much of the director's work in setting the scene.[2] When he was finally able to release the film in the US he scratched Reed's voiceover and had Joseph Cotten, who plays Holly, rerecord it. Out went 'we'd run anything', to be replaced by 'they could get anything if people wanted it enough'. Selznick tried to dispel the air of moral uncertainty that adds an edge to the way Reed's narrator introduces the film's *éminence grise*:

8   Graham Greene (left) and David O. Selznick

> Oh wait, I was going to tell you – I was going to tell you about Holly Martins from America. He came here to visit a friend. The name was Lime, Harry Lime. Now Martins was broke and Lime had offered him – I don't know – some sort of a job. Anyway, there he was, poor chap, happy as a lark and without a cent.

> I was dead broke when I got to Vienna. A close pal of mine had wired me offering me a job doing publicity work for some kind of a charity he was running. I'm a writer, name's Martins, Holly Martins. Anyway, down I came all the way to old Vienna, happy as a lark and without a dime.

Harry Lime's name has gone in Selznick's version. And gone too is that bittersweet, paradoxical 'poor'. *Poor chap, happy as a lark.* Greene ended the novella, which was the basis for his screenplay, with the same sentiment: 'Poor Crabbin. Poor all of us, come to think of it.'[3]

There is the lamentation after all, a sideways glance at the misery of things, the misery you do not see, for better or worse, when you are 'happy as a lark'.

. . . .

As well as changing the voiceover, Selznick made cuts in the American version, dispensing with some unsubtitled German speech and abbreviating the ending. It took fifty years for the British release version of *The Third Man* to be shown widely in the US, and by then Selznick's cut had featured in the American Film Institute's 100 Greatest American Films poll at number fifty-seven. One critic thought its inclusion there a 'colonialist fantasy',[4] but it would be just as misleading to call it simply a British film, given the central involvement of Selznick, Cotten and Orson Welles. However, there is no question that Reed's film has far greater status in British film culture. When, in 2000, the British Film Institute decided to emulate the AFI and poll a host of critics and industry figures to find 'the favourite British films of the 20th Century', *The Third Man* emerged at the top of the list.

It fought off *Brief Encounter* (David Lean, 1945, at number two), *Great Expectations* (Lean, 1946, five), *Kind Hearts and Coronets* (Robert Hamer, 1949, six), *The Red Shoes* (Michael Powell and Emeric Pressburger, 1948, nine), *Brighton Rock* (John Boulting, 1947, fifteen), *Henry V* (Laurence Olivier, 1944, eighteen) and *A Matter of Life and Death* (Powell and Pressburger, 1946, twenty) – that is eight films from a five-year period.

The period from the end of war in Europe in 1944 to, say, 1950 saw an unprecedented flowering of the British film industry and of British film art. This was the Golden Age – if there ever was one. There would be other revivals but none would match the achievements of the immediate post-war years, when Powell and Pressburger were making one outstanding picture after another, kept company by Lean, Olivier and Hamer (to name just the most prominent), and when Reed was being lauded by no less a critic than André Bazin, founder of *Cahiers du Cinéma*, as 'the most brilliant of English directors and one of the foremost in the world'.[5]

. . . .

With his production company London Films' Austrian currency reserves in mind, Korda first had the idea to make a film set in four-power Vienna. 'We want to make a picture in Austria,' Korda told the screenwriter Paul Tabori in 1946.[6] 'It'll be a comedy ... and the basic idea is "invisible frontiers". I want you to do a treatment as quickly as possible.' Nothing came of Tabori's involvement: Korda's thinking took a different turn.

Following the successful development of *The Fallen Idol* (1948), his first film with Greene and Reed, which was then being shot, Korda took the idea to the novelist and pestered him about it until Greene came back with the germ of a story in a single sentence: 'I had paid my last farewell to Harry a week ago, when his coffin was lowered into the frozen February ground, so that it was with incredulity that I saw him pass by, without a sign of recognition, among the host of strangers in the Strand.'[7] Korda was hooked but Greene had trouble moving on. Then, at the end of September 1947, the elaboration of his 'Risen-from-the-dead story' (as he called it[8]) became clearer.

The following February Greene went to Vienna to do research. He was struck by the debris that still littered the city years after the end of Allied bombing and by the cavernous sewer system. A reporter from *The Times*, Peter Smollett, told him about the black market trade in watered-down penicillin, adding another piece to the emerging whole. Greene stayed at Sacher's, the hotel mostly reserved for British officers, and visited various bars and nightclubs (often in the company of Elizabeth Montagu, a German-speaking London Films factotum, and once with fellow novelist Elizabeth Bowen), all of which would find their way into *The Third Man*.

After two weeks he travelled via Prague to Rome where he met his lover Catherine Walston. With the £9,000 Korda had paid him he bought a yacht, the *Nausikaa*, and a villa in Anacapri that was to be a haven for the rest of his life. There he finished the novella that was to be the basis of the new film. He handed it over to Korda in early March.

In April, with *The Fallen Idol* safely out of the way, Korda took Reed to visit Selznick in Bermuda. By the middle of May a deal had been signed for four films. In return for the right to release London Films productions in the US, Selznick would provide finance and access to his rostrum of contracted stars. *The Third Man*, the first film to come under the terms of the deal (Powell and Pressburger's *Gone to Earth* would follow in 1950 before the deal ended acrimoniously in the courts), was green-lit.

Reed and Greene took a further trip to Vienna. They toured the city, then paced out scenes in Reed's hotel room, working out the storyline and continuity. By the time they returned to England a draft script was finished. Selznick had insisted on a provision in his contract with Korda that he be consulted on the script (though he had no right of veto). Reed and Greene duly went to California in August for intensive discussions. Pages and pages of notes were composed, drawing on memos from Selznick and another draft of the script. But the final script barely reflected the American's input.

. . . .

Selznick and Korda wanted Cary Grant to play Holly and Noël Coward to play Harry. Grant was interested but the terms he demanded were prohibitive. Reed objected to Coward but only because he wanted Orson Welles, in the teeth of Selznick's objections and Korda's reservations. The director resorted to unconventional tactics. Tabori recalled how Welles telephoned Reed just as he was speaking on another line to Korda: 'Reed

What might have been:
Cary Grant at Shepperton with
Cotten and Welles

hesitated for a moment – and then he did an "awful thing". He hung up on Alex as if they had been cut off. He talked to Welles and arranged everything amicably. Then he called back Korda in London, pretending that the connection had been broken.'[9] Selznick assigned Cotten and Alida Valli to the production, and the principal cast was completed when Trevor Howard, who had taken a small role in Reed's morale-boosting *The Way Ahead* (1944) and had had a great success in *Brief Encounter*, signed up. Had Welles reneged on his agreement, Howard would have taken on his role.

Cast and crew began work in Vienna at the end of October, staying there for three weeks. The financing was aided by the fact that Korda had taken receipt of £1.2 million on 15 October, this sum being the first part of a subvention from the National Film Finance Corporation, a body which had been set up by the President of the Board of Trade, Harold Wilson, to channel funds into British film production.[10]

It was a typically inclement autumn, with rain, sleet and snow. The rain gave the streets a pleasing sheen, and when it snowed Reed moved filming to the sewers. Much of the photography was done at night by Robert Krasker's first unit. Stan Pavey headed the second unit in the sewers, Hans Schneeberger the third unit (daylight shooting). Studio filming took place in London, first at Isleworth then Shepperton, from December 1948 through to March 1949. At Shepperton Vincent Korda designed the sets, assisted by the backdrop painter Ferdinand Bellan. The Vienna cemetery was recreated there and, in January, when Welles arrived, the Great Wheel interior scenes were filmed with back projection.

Selznick was in London in August to approve a final cut for the European market and *The Third Man* premiered on 2 September to great critical acclaim. But then Korda and Selznick fell out. Back in California Selznick decided to release the film in the US as 'A Selznick Picture'. Korda was furious, though it was not chiefly a matter of pride: he had been hoping to renegotiate their contract, which did not allot him any share of the US box office. And he had a trump card to play, being in possession of the only negative of *The Third Man*. He held out. Selznick had first to cancel the planned release, then concede both the credit (which became 'A Selznick Release') and a share of US box-office receipts. The film finally opened there on 2 February 1950.[11]

. . . .

At his platform gate at Vienna station, Holly is perplexed for an instant when Harry fails to meet him. He makes his way quickly to Stiftgasse 15, a roomy neoclassical apartment block with a great central stair. There is no reply when Holly knocks on his friend's door, but the bustle below draws the attention of the elderly porter (Paul Hoerbiger), who peers down from the stairwell on the next floor. When Holly explains that he understands no German the porter switches to faltering English. (Actually Hoerbiger himself had no English, so Montagu coached him phonetically in Vienna and at the studio.) His eyes twinkle as he wonders whether Harry is in heaven or hell, pointing to the ceiling to indicate the inferno. It is a sharp little joke, an instance of the comedy that, for the most part, will never be far away in *The Third Man*. It takes Holly a while to register the news but finally his sunny look changes.

At the cemetery Major Calloway (Trevor Howard), a military policeman, lounges against a headstone, a little way from the burial service, but within earshot of it. With his pencil moustache and his gleaming leather greatcoat he looks slightly camp.

There is an air of shiftiness. Calloway sizes Holly up out of the corner of his eye and, when they see him, the two Viennese mourners, 'Baron' Kurtz (Ernst Deutsch) and Dr Winkel (Erich Ponto), splendidly got up in furs, do the same. But Holly senses none of this, busy as he is

Loaded glances at Harry's funeral

Paul Hoerbiger is coached by
Elizabeth Montagu – the Austrian
director Paul Martin (left) assists
with translation

casting his own furtive glance at the woman, Anna Schmidt (Valli),
standing in front of him, at the edge of the grave. In her turn Anna's sad
eyes look only at the ceremony or perhaps, because she is jolted when the
priest offers to pass her the shovel of earth, at some vague fixed point that
can hold her gaze while her mind drifts. She has the same steadfast
expression as she walks along the cemetery road. Holly has another peep
at her as he passes in Calloway's car on the way to the bar where the major
has offered to buy him a drink.

....

The 'old Vienna' was a vanishing dream even before World War II. Max
Ophuls explored the fragility of the idea in his 1932 film *Liebelei* (which
has a marvellous role for Hoerbiger as a kind father afraid that his
daughter will never find happiness). Fritz (Wolfgang Liebeneiner) and
Christine (Magda Schneider) fall in love as they walk slowly through the
streets at night, the shots fading in and out, fog tenderly cocooning the
lovers. It is 1910. The officers' dress uniforms symbolise the decadence of
nineteenth-century militarism. A culture of monocles and honour-codes
has begun to rot away. Near the end Ophuls shoots at ground level as the
seconds pace out the perimeter of a duel. The image is desolate: it
betokens impending trench warfare. By the end Fritz and Christine are
both dead, victims of a poisoned social order.

Austria was absorbed into Nazi Germany in 1938. The *Anschluss*
was followed by the *Blitzverfolgung* or 'lightning persecution' of
dissidents. Tens of thousands fled as war loomed. The annexation was
never recognised by the Allied powers; in 1940 Churchill broadcast a call
for the liberation of Austria. In the Moscow declaration of October 1943,

Liebelei: falling in love at
night

which would be reaffirmed at Yalta in February 1945, the three Allied
powers formalised a promise to establish a free and independent Austria.
But there was little that could be done immediately. By July 1942,
Vienna's pre-*Anschluss* Jewish population of some 200,000 had
diminished to 22,000 as a result first of mass emigration, then of mass
murder at Dachau and Buchenwald.[12]

The Red Army crossed the border in April 1945. Commander-in-
Chief Marshal Tolbukhin declared the Soviet intention to respect the
country's integrity and social order. But his troops pillaged, raped and
vandalised. 'At the end of one year of occupation the bitter joke
circulating in Vienna was that Austria could probably survive a third
world war, but it could never endure a second liberation.'[13] Western
troops did not enter Vienna until late August. The city was formally
placed under four-power control on 1 September, in accordance with an
agreement made at Potsdam, the last summit between the victorious
powers to reflect their alliance. The Austrian state treaty, which was a final
adjustment of the fronts of the cold war in Europe, was only signed, in
Vienna, on 15 May 1955.

. . . .

In Bar Smolka on Karntnerstrasse, the Austrian liquor has begun to get to
Holly. He starts to reminisce about Harry but his very first words bring
into question the sincerity of the reminiscence: 'I guess nobody knew
Harry like he did – like I did.' Holly is a novelist, author of trashy pulp
Westerns (*The Lone Rider of Santa Fe*, *Death at Double X Ranch*), 'cheap
novelettes' as Calloway calls them when he stops hiding his disdain, and,
pondering on the death of the friend who rescued him from misery at

school, Holly, like a hard-boiled narrator, instinctively registers the experience in the third person.

Calloway smokes, sneering a little, as he breaks some news about Harry: 'He was about the worst racketeer who ever made a dirty living in this city.' For the first time in the film the camera has begun to be tilted sideways, just a few degrees or so, but noticeably, a gentle introduction to one of the film's major stylistic devices. The technique is unobtrusive for the moment: it seems appropriate given Holly's drunkenness, and it underlines the discord brewing between the two men, which flares up as Holly tries to rebut the broad charges Calloway levels against Harry. The American takes an ineffectual swing at the English major and is rewarded for his trouble with a better-aimed punch from Sergeant Paine (Bernard Lee). 'Take him to Sacher's. Don't hit him again if he behaves,' Calloway says, and Paine is quite happy to do so, being, as it turns out, a fan of Holly's work.

'That's what I like about them, sir, you can pick them up and put them down anytime,' Paine declares, a little unkindly, as he ushers his charge into the lobby of the upmarket hotel commandeered by the British military. Dabbing his cut lip with a handkerchief, Holly is still smarting at Calloway as he signs the register, but quite prepared to follow his instructions and leave on the next day's flight. Paine, though, sees Crabbin (Wilfrid Hyde-White), representative of 'CRS of GHQ', the British 'Cultural Re-education Section', and notifies him that Holly is a writer.

In a film full of terrific cameos, Hyde-White's Crabbin is one of the best. A thin-faced gent, impeccably dressed and no doubt thoroughly clubbable, Crabbin puts on the CRS's 'shows': it was *Hamlet* the week before, he tells Holly, and Hindu dancers before that (or 'the striptease', as Paine calls it), but they have never had the opportunity of welcoming an American author. Holly shows no interest until Crabbin makes it clear

At Bar Smolka and Sacher's

that the CRS will put him up for as long as he likes if he agrees to speak at the Institute. There is still time to clear Harry's name.

So the wind is back in Holly's sails when, a few moments later, he takes a call from 'Baron' Kurtz and agrees to a meeting at the Café Mozart not far from the hotel.

....

Fast bonds of friendship underpinned the production. For Alexander and Vincent Korda, his brother, it was a family affair. Vincent's son, the publisher Michael Korda, in a memoir, *Charmed Lives*, noted in addition the feelings for Reed: 'Carol … Alex genuinely came to love, and it was difficult to say which one of them had adopted the other.'[14]

Greene also became close to Reed. On 21 June 1948, during their visit to Vienna, he wrote to Catherine Walston from the Astoria: 'I am getting terribly bored with … everybody except Carol who gets nicer and nicer on acquaintance.'[15] The impression was only strengthened and Greene placed this dedication at the front of the published edition of the novella: 'TO CAROL REED / in admiration and affection / and in memory of so many early morning / Vienna hours at Maxim's, the Casanova, / the Oriental.' The writer even had time for the troublesome co-producer. In California on 9 August he wrote to Elizabeth Montagu: 'All my prejudices are confirmed, except that I like Selznick enormously.'[16]

A still stronger affection existed between Greene and Korda. In *Ways of Escape* (1980) the novelist noted that only one of his principal characters had ever been modelled on someone he knew: 'Dreuther, the business tycoon in *Loser Takes All* [1955], is undeniably Alexander Korda,

Cotten, Reed and Howard drinking in Vienna

and the story remains important to me because it is soaked in memories of Alex, a man whom I loved.' 'How he penetrated my life,' he went on.[17]

It is important to stress the atmosphere of cordial collaboration that undoubtedly prevailed during the production, with everyone playing to their strengths. But this is not to downplay Reed's claim to authorship. It is instead to specify a feature of his skill as a director: he had a gift for friendship and co-operation. Actors, in particular, loved to work with him. Michael Redgrave said that he 'learned for the first time how intimate the relationship between actor and director could be'.[18] James Mason concurred: 'Carol Reed was my favourite director. Before *Odd Man Out* I had never worked with him but in every one of his films I had seen there was great warmth and understanding.'[19] So did Peter Ustinov: 'Carol Reed's greatness lies not in his technical virtuosity, but in his natural sympathy with the actor.'[20]

This gift of Reed's must have been crucial for *The Third Man*. Trevor Howard summed it up: 'It was a wonderful time. Wouldn't have missed it for the world. I loved making that film.'[21]

It is, after all, not so common a gift.

. . . .

Male friendship is one of the central themes of *The Third Man*, a theme made rich and poignant by the pairing of Welles and Cotten, who had first met in 1936. But, in contrast to the relationships behind the scenes, friendship is always at risk in the film and it has been claimed that homosexuality is a major factor in the sense of instability.

It all began with Greene's decision to call his protagonist – an Englishman in the novella – 'Rollo Martins'. When Cotten saw the name he objected. Greene recalled the episode in *Ways of Escape*:

> Joseph Cotten quite reasonably objected to my choice of name, Rollo in the story, which to his American ear apparently involved homosexuality. I wanted the name none the less to be an absurd one, and the name Holly occurred to me when I remembered that figure of fun, the nineteenth-century American poet Thomas Holley Chivers.[22]

Greene's 'quite reasonably' here is sarcastic, but even so scholars, among them Greene's biographer Michael Shelden, have sought to find a homosexual subtext. 'Harry is no ordinary friend,' according to Shelden, 'Martins's attitude is almost like that of a lover who cannot decide whether to end a bad affair.'[23]

He was not the first to make this inference. When Greene came to London's National Film Theatre in 1984 to be interviewed by Quentin Falk, he remembered a conversation with Selznick: 'he went on to say, "And what's all this buggery, boys? What's all this buggery?" I said, "Buggery"? He said, "Look. Chap goes out to find his friend. Doesn't find him. He's apparently dead. Why doesn't he go home?"'[24] The producer's concerns cannot have been much allayed, because he reverted to the same theme again on 25 October 1948, just as shooting was about to get under way: 'what on earth motivates Martins in his curious and passionate interest in clearing up the reputation of a dead man who he *hasn't seen for ten years*. ... The only conclusion I can draw from it is that they slept together, and I don't mean slept, all the way through Eton.'[25]

On the face of it, Selznick's concern seems crazy and obsessive. Some archival papers, however, modify that initial impression. In the Carol Reed collection in the BFI's Special Collections there is a typewritten minute of a conference, dated 17 August 1948, in which Selznick made comments on the script. One item reads: 'Chg reference to Carter having slept with Martins.' On the next page of the 'Conference Notes' another remark is recorded: 'No hint of homo-sexuality.'[26]

There are also three versions of the script in the collection, one of which, undated and marked 'DRAFT', is surely the version Selznick had seen in early August. It includes a brief scene in which Calloway is speaking to Carter on the phone. 'Somebody's been talking to your Sleeping Partner about Harben,'[27] he says.

Who is this Carter? Turn back a few pages of the script and there is this extraordinary, hilarious scene at Sacher's:

MARTINS' BEDROOM (NIGHT)
Martins is half undressed and is lying on the outside of his bed, with his shoes on. He is wide awake and staring at the ceiling. The door opens and Captain Carter, a young tough phlegmatic officer, appears, carrying a valise.
CARTER: Hullo. What are you doing here?
MARTINS: It's my room.
CARTER: As a matter of fact it's mine.
He begins to unpack his valise.
MARTINS: Are you Carter?
CARTER: Yes. Seen a sponge about?
MARTINS: On the chest of drawers.

CARTER: Thought I'd lost it. Thanks.
MARTINS: They said you were in Klagenfurt. What shall I do. There isn't another room.
CARTER: The bed's big enough for two. (He picks up the telephone and dials). Do you snore?
MARTINS: No.
CARTER: Nor do I.[28]

Carter makes a call to Calloway (still, as in the novella, a colonel), which is interrupted briefly by another call, from Kurtz, who wants to meet Holly. The soldiers' conversation resumes, with Calloway acerbically warning his subordinate that the American 'hits people'. At the end of the scene Carter 'turns towards Martins, who is lying on the bed staring up at the ceiling. Carter watches him suspiciously, feels the springs on the bed, and starts to undress – Dissolve.'

This belatedly written scene accomplishes no real dramatic business – in the film Holly simply takes Kurtz's call in the hotel lobby – and even if it did it is overelaborated. So what is it doing here? Did Greene write it just to get under Selznick's skin?

. . . .

Holly never got to bed down with tough young Carter. Instead he hurried to the Mozart. With the cut from Sacher's to the square outside the café, the zither music starts up again, a sedate waltz that has just the right tempo to accompany the image of Kurtz strolling up to the tables set out on the pavement. His ease seems studied, like the flash of a smile when he sees Holly. To his right lapel he clasps a copy of *Oklahoma Kid* and a close-up shows the cover. It is perhaps no surprise that the edition seems cheap, without a dust jacket, the cover-image – a neckerchiefed cowboy with a revolver in each hand, two red aces flung into the air to his left – artless and hackneyed. But Kurtz is polite enough, admiring the suspenseful ending of each chapter.

The self-styled baron has a suggestive vulpine face. He wants to ingratiate himself, smiling wistfully as he tries to dampen Holly's suspicions, and indeed, with his enveloping fur collar and dotted bow-tie, he has a little of the clown about him, the clown's sad good humour, the clown's cruelty.

That complicated face dissolves into the street outside Harry's apartment where Kurtz runs through the details of the fatal accident while the porter sweeps in the doorway. Kurtz was with Harry when, in response to the greeting of a friend, a Romanian called Popescu, he crossed the road and was hit by a truck. His dying words, Kurtz says, were reserved for Holly. The porter has been watching the two men talk across the street and now Holly walks over to him, remembering that he said Harry had died instantly.

While Kurtz was talking he held up a tiny dog in his elegantly gloved hand. Whatever impression of gentleness that might have given is dispelled by the cutaway to him. He looks unguardedly malevolent. Holly hardly has the chance to question the porter before his matronly wife (Annie Rosar) calls him inside insistently, pleading a telephone call. Holly is left with Kurtz.

The baron gives up two further pieces of information. He can be found in the evenings at the Casanova Club. And the woman at the funeral is performing at the Josefstadt theatre. Kurtz tries to dissuade Holly from visiting her – 'it would only cause her pain' – but sees that it is no good. So the baron changes tack, fulsomely friendly again, gushing about how good it was to meet 'a master of suspense', and complimenting him on that terrible cover.

....

Before going on general release in the UK in October 1949, *The Third Man* was shown in competition at Cannes; it won the festival's first Grand Prix. The wrangles over the American release scuppered its chances at the 1950 Academy Awards, but Krasker was garlanded with the award for cinematography. And, a few weeks earlier, Selznick accepted (on Reed's behalf) the Critics' Award of New York film writers.

Reed and Korda admire the diploma and landscape painting presented to mark the Cannes award

Critical reaction was overwhelmingly favourable in all parts of the press.[29] The mass-market *Daily Mirror* (2 September 1949) ran the headline 'Pardon Me if I Rave!' above its critic Reg Whitley's notice: 'The film combines superb artistry with 100 per cent entertainment value … a magnificent piece of screencraft!' The *Cambridge Daily News* (25 October) concurred: 'Don't be misled by any high-falutin' ideas you might have conjured-up about Mr. Reed. Certainly he is a director who believes in the cinema as a medium of artistic expression … but at the same time he has not missed the beat of the public's pulse.' The same theme was taken up in the *Mail* (2 September): 'What is the secret of this man, who has the approval of the highbrows … and still gives the ninepennies a storming entertainment?'

American critics, reviewing the film in the first week of February 1949, were equally warm. 'Probably American filmgoers' best of 1950' (*Time*); 'Carol Reed is a picture Titan of genius. This is pioneer photography and story-telling' (*New York Daily Mirror*); 'Profoundly satisfying' (*New York Post*); 'A stunning production' (*New York Daily News*).

Dissenting voices were rare. The British communist paper the *Daily Worker* (3 September 1949) lamented that 'no effort is spared to make the Soviet authorities as sinister and unsympathetic as possible'. Interestingly, the critics who most qualified their admiration for *The Third Man* were also some of the most eminent. Dilys Powell of the *Sunday Times* was one: 'It is, I suppose, because Reed's exceptional talent leads one to expect miracles that I feel a shade of disappointment at the reappearance of the familiar trick and the familiar situation' (4 September 1949). C. A. Lejeune used a similar phrase: 'Mr. Reed has never before elaborated his style so desperately, nor used so many tricks in the presentation of a film' (*Observer*, 4 September).

The suggestion of trickery echoed across the Atlantic in the piece by Bosley Crowther, on his way to becoming the Grand Old Man of American middlebrow film reviewing. 'It is just a bang-up melodrama, designed to excite and entertain,' he huffed and puffed, before adding that 'Mr. Reed has brilliantly packaged the whole bag of his cinematic tricks' (*New York Times*, 3 February 1950).

....

At the theatre Holly is bemused by the mannered farce unfolding on the stage. He slips backstage and gets a whispered 'afterwards' from Anna when he tells her from the wings that he was a friend of Harry Lime.

A little later they swap pleasantries in her dressing room. As they do so Anna removes her wig and theatrical eyelashes, then combs the wig as she smokes a cigarette. They compare notes. Anna recalls that Kurtz brought her money after Harry's death, apparently in fulfilment of his dying wish, and she mentions Dr Winkel, whom Harry consulted, who was passing the scene of the accident. At the inquest, she adds, Harry's driver was exonerated.

'I don't get it. All of them there: Kurtz, this Romanian Popescu, his own driver knocking him over, his own doctor just passing by. No strangers there at all.'

'I know,' says Anna, without much apparent feeling, 'I wondered about it a hundred times, if it really was an accident.'

The zitherist has been minding his own business, desultory too, but as soon as Anna has spoken there is an outburst, a quick flurry of vehemently plucked notes that accompanies a cut to Holly turning around and looking at Anna with vexation and alarm. The playing subsides again but there is new animation in it. Holly asks Anna if she knows the porter. It is on account of those moments of acceleration in the music, rather than anything in the acting, that the narrative is suddenly charged.

Anna at the Josefstadt; Holly questions the porter while Anna remembers Harry

The sideways tilts were becoming more frequent during Holly's visit to the Josefstadt and, after the dissolve from Anna unfastening her costume behind a screen to the porter opening the street-facing window in Harry's apartment, the technique imposes itself definitively on the film. As the porter remembers the accident, the clockwise tilt is emphasised by the skewed shadows cast by the slats of the window in the top portion of the screen and, at its extreme right, by the misaligned edge of the window frame. Hoerbiger, with his slicked-back, luxuriant full head of silver hair, is charming again, his demonstrative hands compensating for his broken English.

As Holly questions him the camera leaves them and the zither returns in a casual but melancholy mood to mark Anna's return to her lover's apartment. She sits in front of the bedroom mirror, having taken a comb from Harry's drawer, and tends her hair. The scene moves in different directions at once, one element of its composition (Holly's urgent search for the truth) playing off another (Anna's quiet commemoration of Harry) without cancelling it out. This is beautiful film-making, characteristic of *The Third Man*, because it conjures up an indefinite mood, mixing up noir-like investigation with melodramatic emotion.[30]

Holly is finding contradictions and inconsistencies. The porter insists that Harry was 'quite dead' on impact; he becomes agitated. The fact is that he chose not to speak up at the inquest. But he was not the only one. 'There was a third man. He didn't give evidence.' The phone rings and Anna answers, taking dice from a box on the bedside table as she does so, but gets no reply. The dice are a slightly awkward touch but the point is that Anna reaches for them as a reflex: she has done so many times before. Holly presses the porter, telling him he has to go to the police, and the porter's patience snaps. He has always liked Anna, he tells her, but this is none of his business and he does not want to see the foreigner in the building again.

As he delivers his agitated speech, he tosses a rubber ball back to the puffy-faced little child (Herbert Halbik) dressed in a beret, short trousers and knee-length overcoat who had appeared in the doorway a few moments before, and had been looking and listening intently ever since.

. . . .

In May 1948, before they came to Vienna, Cotten and Valli acted together in an undistinguished B-picture, *Walk Softly, Stranger*, directed by Robert Stevenson, which was only released in 1950 in an attempt to profit from *The Third Man*'s success.[31]

Cotten is Chris Hale, a good-natured gambler and thief, who falls in love with Valli's Elaine Corelli, an heiress crippled after a ski-jumping accident in St Moritz. Eventually his past catches up with him. Before he is jailed, Elaine visits him. The film's closing lines are hers: 'When you come back you'll be changed, you'll be hurt too, then maybe you'll need me. In whatever life you try to find, please find me too because I belong to you.' The scene is inadvertently hilarious. *By going to prison*, Elaine says, *you can be a martyr too! Walk Softly, Stranger* is turgid and preachy and neither lead can fight their way out of it. Stevenson should have watched how Alfred Hitchcock had used these actors.

Hitchcock could deliberately limit actresses but, more often, he liked, so to speak, to set them in a trap. This is what he did with Valli in *The Paradine Case* (1947, produced by Selznick, who also wrote the screenplay). For much of the film, suspected of murdering her wealthy husband, Maddalena Anna Paradine is vacant and closed to persuasion or interrogation. Then her defence lawyer (Gregory Peck) accidentally forces her to confess in court. That passive face fills with implacable rage. Finally the hatred is replaced by sorrow. Even when emotion overtakes her, though, there is a sense of reserve. Valli's appeal as a film actress, which Hitchcock recognised, had to do with her ability to resist disclosing too much of a character – or to disclose only as if under duress and then with brutality, lashing out when there is no other way of protecting some

immeasurably private core.

Hitchcock sought out the darkness in Cotten also. In *Shadow of a Doubt* (1942), the director's favourite film, he plays a serial killer who goes to ground with his sister and her family. He is all charm at first, but as time goes by his contempt begins to show itself. In a bar with his niece Charlie (Theresa Wright), it bursts out: 'How do you know what the world is like? Do you know the world is a foul sty? Do you know if you rip the fronts off houses you'd find swine? The world's a hell – what does it matter what happens in it?'

Cotten and Valli strike a stiff pose for a *Walk Softly, Stranger* production still

Valli's face full of rage in
The Paradine Case …

… and then full of sorrow

'Do you know the world is
a foul sty?'

There is no mistaking Hitchcock's interest, because he revived it more intricately in *Under Capricorn* (1949, shot that summer). Cotten is Sam Flusky, a former convict who, in 1931 Sydney, has become a wealthy recluse. Resentment and guilt have eaten him away. In one remarkable shot, a huge close-up, he towers up, his face a maelstrom of emotion that seems about to explode out of him.

In fact *Under Capricorn* ends in redemption. It is one of Hitchcock's finest films, much neglected, and in it Cotten is brilliant and complex – as he tended to be when playing a character whom chaos or despair threaten to overwhelm. Negative feelings electrify him as an actor. And likewise the fire in Valli is only really visible when her character begins to hate and avenge.

. . . .

Anna returns home with Holly only to be informed by her elderly landlady (Hedwig Bleibtreu) that the police are searching her flat. The landlady keeps out the cold by draping herself in a quilt and railing against the occupying troops.

Inside, Calloway, wearing a duffle coat, is as assured as ever. Despite Holly's jeers and protests, but not without a certain tenderness,

Anna's landlady protests in vain; Calloway and Paine inspect Anna's false papers; Anna's face is a mask

27

he confiscates Anna's Austrian papers along with love letters from Harry. Anna seems to have no resistance in her. She half-heartedly tries to keep back the letters but Paine says, 'we're used to it, like doctors'.

The scene is carefully blocked. Anna falls back as Holly pesters Calloway (or 'Callaghan' as he persists in calling him) about Harry's death, then he falls back himself as Anna goes up to the major and more or less admits that her papers are forged: 'Harry never did anything, only a small thing once, out of kindness', indicating the papers.

At the military police HQ Anna is left alone in Calloway's office and she looks out through its glass-paned wall to see his Russian counterpart Brodsky (Alexis Chesnakov) inspecting her papers with relish and purpose.

. . . .

When he shot *Odd Man Out* (1947) in Belfast, Reed took care to use both local people and some fine Irish actors, several of whom were part of the great Abbey Theatre company in Dublin. The unknown extras and the professionals together contributed significantly to the film's sense of place.

It was the same with *The Third Man*. Highly accomplished Austrian or German actors were cast as Harry's friends, the porter and the landlady. None of the actors would have been recognisable to audiences unfamiliar with German and Austrian cinema – except, perhaps, Ernst Deutsch, born in Prague in 1890, who worked in Hollywood, in small roles, in the 1930s and 1940s, taking on the screen name 'Ernest Dorian' in 1942 or so.

But these were actors with hundreds and hundreds of stage and screen credits between them. Paul Hoerbiger (more usually Hörbiger), for example, born in Budapest in 1894, made a clutch of films every year from the late 1920s to the mid-60s. His last screen credit came in 1972; he died in Vienna in 1981, aged eighty-six. Erich Ponto, from Lübeck in Germany, came late to the cinema in 1930, when he was in his mid-forties, but had a busy career thereafter, right up to his death in 1957. Siegfried Breuer, a native of Vienna, died young at the age of forty-seven but at the time had some forty-six screen credits. He excelled at 'playing unreliable types: most memorably as the seducer in one of the best films of the Nazi era, *Der Postmeister* [Gustav Ucicky, 1940]'.[32] Hedwig Bleibtreu, 'an actress who was venerated as one of the erstwhile *grandes dames* of the Viennese stage',[33] born in the Austrian town of Linz in 1868, hardly worked in the cinema until 1930 but then appeared regularly until a few years before her death in Vienna, aged eighty-nine, in 1958.

It makes a difference that these smaller roles were played by such talented professionals. They are able to dazzle without much effort and without distracting from the main characters. Their skill, though, has another quality. It gives a strong impression of potential, unexploited ability, as if the actors, while remaining impeccably polite, were not going to give away too much of themselves in the presence of strangers. This quality of the acting adds to the depiction of an occupied city whose citizens have had to learn to watch their words.

The Third Man never pretends to have comprehensive knowledge of its Vienna. Instead it emphasises its limited viewpoint, its lack of local understanding, its foreignness – therefore the deliberately contrived camerawork, which makes the city locations seem forbidding. So also the decision to include unsubtitled German speech in the film, which acts as a

Breuer in *Der Postmeister*

Bleibtreu with the actress Maria Schell at Shepperton

barrier to the audience. The non-German-speaking spectator is at times made to feel like a tourist, Holly or a disgruntled foreign military policeman. It adds just a little more to the feeling of uneasiness.

And it is important that much of the German speech is in fact complaint at foreigners. When Holly interrogates him too insistently about Harry's death, the porter loses his patience: '*Ach, jetzt hat's aber zwölfe g'schlagn – mich lass'ns aus mit der Polizei. Das hat man davon, wenn ma freundlich is mit de Ausländer*' – 'Oh, now, that's just too much – I've had enough of the police. This is what comes of being friendly to a foreigner.' Later on the landlady protests to Holly at Calloway's search of Anna's apartment: '*Sie sind Amerikaner. Wär so etwas in Ihrem Lande möglich? Die Leute benehmen sich ja wie die Einbrecher. Eines ist sicher – die Befreiung hab ich mir ganz anders vorgestellt*' – 'You are American. Would this be possible in your country? These people take things away just like they were burglars. One thing is for sure – I thought the liberation was going to be very different.'

....

It is still night and there is condensation on Holly's breath as he walks up to Dr Winkel's house. A close-up of a well-garnished roast goose is enough to suggest that the occupant enjoys luxuries that are rare in this deprived city. Hilde (Jenny Werner), the housekeeper, reluctantly lets Holly in after the doctor instructs her to do so. Holly steps from the hallway into an ornate parlour cum consulting room (a hygienic-looking bed is in one corner) adorned with religious relics.

Ponto's Dr Winkel is sly and aloof but somehow supercilious too. He cannot help it that Holly recognises Kurtz's little dog when it makes its way, yelping a little as it does, into the parlour from the dining room – but otherwise he obfuscates as much as he can. He lies fluently when Holly asks

Feigned good feeling: Winkel and Brodsky

him about the dog and he hardly shows any agitation, except perhaps when he caresses the wick of a candle between his thumb and second finger or blows on the shoulder of a figurine (though no dust seems to be there). But nothing suggests that he finds Holly's investigations threatening.

A little later, at the four-power HQ, Anna watches Brodsky take a vaguely sadistic delight in her forged passport. He asks Calloway to keep hold of it while he conducts some enquiries. All the same, Anna asks the major if she can have it back. He is more interested in what he has gleaned from Harry's letters and questions her about one Joseph Harbin, who works at a military hospital, perhaps the same 'Joseph', Calloway suggests, whom Anna telephoned with a message from Harry (relayed to her in one of the letters). Harbin has since disappeared. Anna balks at each question, protesting her ignorance: 'you've got everything upside down.' Calloway looks unconvinced but he has no more to say and instead he draws her attention to Holly who, below them, is standing impatiently on the pavement as a tramcar curves past: 'That American friend of yours is still waiting for you. He won't do you much good.'

....

At the time he made *The Third Man*, Reed kept a small zoo in his Chelsea home, as Michael Korda remembered it. An aviary took up a whole wall in his drawing room. He kept a hedgehog. 'Occasionally he chose the wrong kind of pet, as was the case when his two cranes made their way up the fire escape of a nearby house, causing great consternation when they appeared in the bathroom of an elderly lady.'[34] Reed's love of animals is reflected in his films. In *The Fallen Idol* the most decisive proof of the

Two uncredited members of the cast travel in style

malevolence of Mrs Baines (Sonia Dresdel) comes when she incinerates MacGregor, the little grass snake cherished by Felipe (Bobby Henrey), in a stove. There are three animals in *The Third Man* – Kurtz's miniature dog, Anna's cat and the cockatoo in the British cultural centre. Each of them is hostile to Holly, as if they smell some threat coming off him.

. . . .

A dissolve reveals the neon sign of the Casanova Revuebuhne Bar. As Holly and Anna go in, who should they be met by but Mr Crabbin? He is accompanied, as he was at Sacher's, by an elegant female companion who, unaccountably, shuffles quickly out of the door, as if shrinking away from something. Crabbin confirms that the lecture – on 'the crisis of faith' in the modern novel – has been arranged for the next day.

Anna sits at the bar, a picture of melancholy. She pays for two whiskies because the club does not take Holly's 'army money'. Kurtz is there too, a dinner-jacketed minstrel in the plush dining area, playing his violin into the ear of a corpulent, bejewelled woman with an overhanging lower lip who eats soup with an air of disgruntlement. When he sees them he stops the music as quickly as he can, sharply plucking two notes to alert another man sitting by the wall with a newspaper. 'You have found out my little secret,' Kurtz, gracefully embarrassed, says to Anna. 'A man must live.'

The baron begins to poke around. Was Dr Winkel not helpful? Holly's suspicions are growing but he is more than pleased to hear that Popescu is in the Casanova even as they speak. Whereas Winkel and Kurtz are weasel-like and calculating, Popescu is garrulous but seedy. With his brilliantined hair and the drooping eyelids and moustache, there is something lecherous about him, a touch of the pimp. He has the scent of the underworld on him in a way the other two do not. But he is not

Popescu dissembles while Anna is lost in thought

sinister or threatening, not yet anyway, and his little asides – the way he makes a meal of berating the waiter for not putting enough ice in Holly's whisky, his faintly embarrassed confession of acid indigestion – are beautifully nuanced, Breuer adding grace notes to character business.

Popescu barely flinches as Holly comes out slugging. 'Who was the third man? ... I was told that a third man helped you and Kurtz carry the body.' Instead he thinks fast: 'Who could have told you a story like that?'

Holly, enjoying his whisky, does not know or care what he is saying when he replies that it was the porter. So the Romanian can turn the charm back on, gently tutting that the porter should have come forward with his testimony: 'You'll never teach these Austrians to be good citizens.'

Holly asks if Popescu knows a man called 'Harbin ... Joseph Harbin'. Presumably Anna has told him about Calloway's questioning. Popescu, in a reverse shot, looks intently away for a second to take in Anna. Suddenly his manner changes. There is harshness in his voice now: 'That's a nice girl, that, but she ought to go careful in Vienna. Everybody ought to go careful in a city like this.'

The same frantic, discordant flurry of notes from the zither that was first heard in Anna's dressing room ratchets up the tension.

. . . .

Anton Karas played for the guests at a welcoming party in Vienna; Reed heard the music and had Karas tracked down. Initially the idea was simply to have some incidental music, and recordings were made for that purpose. But the sound worked its way more and more into Reed's mind. Back in London, he brought Karas over and had him play in front of a Moviola, which showed rushes. Further recordings were then made at Shepperton – though Reed felt the sound was less gritty than he would have wanted – and bit by bit all thought of any other, orchestral music was abandoned.

Karas's music was a one-off, despite its huge popularity: there would be no more zither film scores, and so the sound of the instrument is inextricably tied in most people's minds to *The Third Man*. Karas practised and predetermined certain themes, but the effect on screen of the music is that he is improvising, laying down moods and tempos under the action to reinforce it.

As film music the zither-playing has two essential qualities, quite apart from its uniqueness. It is versatile and it is responsive. Sometimes the music is relaxed and soothing, then all of a sudden it can suggest violence and terror, 'a plangent horror', as William Whitebait had it in his

New Statesman notice (10 September 1949). But the versatility is part of an organic whole. Whitebait referred to 'that orchestral handling of image, talk, and music that one has looked for, so often in vain, since its early apparition in *Sous les toits de Paris* [René Clair, 1930]. The happy convergence staggers us again and again in *The Third Man*.'

Is this right, though? There is another side to the music. In one sense it clings to the contours of the film, but in another sense it is an independent line of meaning, even a countercurrent. In a brilliant (if somewhat disparaging) review, the great American critic Manny Farber used a weird, striking image to describe the zither-playing: it 'hits one's consciousness like a cloudburst of sewing needles'.[35] The sense is that there is something alien or even aggressive about the music. In *Films and Feelings* (1967) Raymond Durgnat specified what this might be:

> Background music is an outrage against realism, but, when creatively used, can have an effect as powerful as the visual images. In *The Third Man* and François Truffaut's *Tirez sur le pianiste* (1960) zither and piano add their own colour to the atmosphere created by the visuals – expressing life's, fate's, bitter, mocking indifference to the characters.[36]

It is at any rate an interesting idea that Karas's music is an inseparable accompaniment to the film and also a cruel riposte; and certainly a strangeness lingers in it, which can be heard when it is listened to on its own.

Karas playing (above), and with Reed in the rerecording studio at Shepperton

There was no initial provision for Karas to receive a royalty for his music, but, when recordings and sales and sheet music went through the roof at the end of 1949, London Films rectified this, giving him fifty per cent of net receipts. He further benefited from long sell-out tours in Europe and America in 1949 and 1950, during which he played to the king and queen of England as well as the pope. With the proceeds he bought a bar in Vienna, which he named after the film that had made him, briefly, such a star.[37]

. . . .

Popescu nearly fills the screen, sternly speaking into the phone: 'He will meet us at the bridge.' The image dissolves quickly to Kurtz surreptitiously emerging from a doorway, then to Winkel, wrapped up against the cold of the early morning, a black-clad gnome dwarfed by his bicycle, its shiny handlebars like antlers. Finally Popescu himself emerges, his eyes hardening as he looks left and right for any sign of unwanted attention.

On the Reichsbrucke four men join in conspiratorial discussion some way off from the skulking camera. That there are four can be clearly seen after the next cut, to a vantage-point near the apex of the bridge's downward-curving upper strut: four tiny figures strolling in the crisp morning air.

Holly is pacing out some vague re-enactment of the accident outside Harry's building, observed (if the logic of the editing is to be countenanced) by the grizzled racketeer who was first seen during the opening montage. From a window above, the porter calls out to his indefatigable visitor: 'Is it so very important for you? … I am not a bad man. I'd like to tell you something. … Come tonight: my wife goes out.' Holly, peering up at the old Austrian, would carry on talking but he is silenced with a gesture.

A cut relocates the camera inside the room with the porter as he turns from closing the inner shutter to be startled by the sight of someone who must have just entered. The porter's face is framed in close-up as the zither jangles in alarm. His features hardly move but his eyes register first shock then fear.

. . . .

The canted camera in *The Third Man* was almost certainly influenced by one of the episodes in Julien Duvivier's *Un carnet de bal* (1937). A squalid dockside garret is occupied by a half-blind abortionist (Pierre Blanchar), whom the widow (Marie Bell), intent on tracking down all the men who

The tilted camera in *Un carnet de bal*

paid suit to her at her first ball, visits. Duvivier's camera is not only tilted during this episode: it rocks from side to side. Greene reviewed Duvivier's film for *Night and Day*, and his evocation is intensely vivid:

> in one episode we have Duvivier's real greatness – the seedy doctor at Marseilles so used to furtive visitors and illegal operations that he doesn't wait for questions before he lights the spirit flame: the dreadful cataracted eye: the ingrained dirt upon his hands: the shrewish wife picked up in God knows what low music-hall railing behind bead curtains: the continuous shriek and grind of winch and crane. Nostalgia, sentiment, regret: the padded and opulent emotions wither before the evil detail: the camera shoots at a slant so that the dingy flat rears like a sinking ship. You have to struggle to the door, but you can run downhill to the medical couch and the bead curtains.[38]

Not everyone approved of Krasker's tilts. Apparently William Wyler, on seeing *The Third Man*, mailed Reed a spirit level with a message reading: 'Carol, next time you make a picture, just put it on top of the camera, will you?'[39] And the tilts have been criticised by reviewers. Jonathan Rosenbaum, for example, has been dismissive: 'shadows equal mystery and skullduggery, tilted angles mean everything's slightly off-kilter. It's a loose strategy for depicting the rubble-strewn Vienna of that period.'[40]

And yet everyone remembers the tilts along with the deep chiaroscuro and the night-time city scenes (shot night for night, often after the streets had been hosed down specially to improve the effects of

Reed and Krasker look
through a viewfinder
during filming of
Odd Man Out

contrast). Krasker's achievement was to create 'some of the most inspired atmospheric lighting achieved on location in the history of the cinema', according to Duncan Petrie. 'Much of the effect was created by the augmentation of natural light sources which provided the combination of strong highlights and long looming shadows among the grand old buildings of Vienna, the mounds of rubble, and down in the sewers';[41] Krasker deserved his Academy Award.

. . . .

Anna is lost in thought, toying with a bedknob, when Holly arrives with news of his evening meeting. Her unhappiness is palpable. Harry used to come by around 6.00, she says, and it is always a 'bad time'.

'I've been frightened, I've been alone, without friends and money – but I've never known anything like this. Please talk. Tell me about him.' As she and Holly exchange banal anecdotes about Harry's resourcefulness, she is soon vibrant and delighted. Delighted not least by Harry's childishness: 'He never grew up. The world grew up round him, that's all – and buried him.' Her ardour puts Holly off: he wants to flirt not to celebrate. So as they both head out of Anna's apartment for the meeting with the porter he is offended by a blatant indication that she is in no way so fickle – she unthinkingly calls him 'Harry'.

Night has fallen and outside the apartment building a small crowd has gathered next to an ambulance. It disconcerts Anna, but Holly presses on. He questions the bystanders but cannot understand them until, one after the other, two men explain that the porter has been murdered – 'kaput', each one says, drawing a finger across his neck. One of them is

father to the boy whose ball rolled into Harry's apartment, and there is Hansl, crisscrossed ball in his mittened hands, his hairless, porcine face animated. (Another familiar face is also glimpsed in this scene – that of the anonymous racketeer.) The boy tugs at his father's sleeve when he sees Holly, determined to cast suspicion on him, but the adults are farcically slow to respond. There is plenty of time for Holly to hurry away with Anna. Hansl, calling out for 'Papa' with grisly relish, trots after them at the head of an ineffectual mob.

A foggy comedy envelops this scene but there is no escaping the fact that the porter is dead. His body, wrapped in a blanket, is briefly seen being wheeled out on a trolley by a paramedic in a white coat. As it passes out on to the street, his wife is also visible, huddled against the doorframe, her face shocked and numb.

. . . .

Reed's films of this period are unusual in being full of interesting children. There is the quiet girl with one rollerskate in *Odd Man Out*, as well as the wonderful urchin after a penny or a cigarette. There is the unspeakable Nina Almayer (Annabel Morley), shouting 'pig!' at her father's instigation in *Outcast of the Islands* (1951). Most touching of all is Horst (Dieter Krause), the boy on a bicycle running errands for Ivo Kern (James Mason) in *The Man Between* (1953), doting on him, intensely and solemnly, and then causing his death because he cannot pass up on a last glimpse of his hero.

Hansl is no less memorable and scary. In the novella, where he is called 'Hansel', he has a 'scrutinizing cold-blooded gnome-gaze' and his 'suspicion and alertness spread like a cloud over the city'.[42] There are other children like him in Greene's work, such as the whisky priest's daughter in *The Power and the Glory* (1940), with her chilling avid stare.

Hansl means to implicate Holly in the porter's murder

He caught the look in the child's eyes which frightened him – it was again as if a grown woman was there before her time, making her plans, aware of far too much. … The child suddenly laughed again knowingly. The seven-year-old body was like a dwarf's: it disguised an ugly maturity.[43]

These children are grotesque, but childhood for Greene is an Eden full of serpents, not grass snakes, and 'ugly maturity' comes with survival.

Both Hansl and Horst are dangerous innocents, like Felipe in *The Fallen Idol*, who nearly ruins everything for his beloved Baines (Ralph Richardson) by being first too honest about what he thinks he knows, then too secretive. Greene and Reed shared the idea that innocence is almost always perilous. To cling on to innocence and idealism beyond childhood, assuming it is even possible, is, for both of them, to court disaster and to ignore the harsh reality of the world. The theme is very clear in Greene's 1955 novel *The Quiet American*:

Pyle had been silent a long while, and I had nothing more to say. Indeed I had said too much. He looked white and beaten and ready to

The urchin, the girl with one rollerskate, Nina, Horst (clockwise from top left)

faint, and I thought, 'What's the good? he'll always be innocent, you can't blame the innocent, they are always guiltless. All you can do is control them or eliminate them. Innocence is a kind of insanity.'[44]

The Quiet American is a high-stakes work, where the earlier novella is an 'entertainment', but there is no mistaking Pyle for anything other than a descendant of Holly Martins.

....

Greene admired Fritz Lang. *Fury* (1936) was a particular favourite. The admiration must have been mutual: Lang adapted Greene's *Ministry of Fear* in 1943.

Another reason why the quasi-comic scene outside Harry's apartment block is disturbing is that it recalls Lang's *M* (1931), in which a man is surrounded on a pavement and nearly lynched because he seems to be accosting a young girl. With undue haste the passers-by suspect him of being the serial killer at loose in Berlin. The panic, vigilantism and violence in *M* hover behind the scene with Hansl, whose shadow, as he runs after Holly and Anna, falls on a wall adorned with posters in the same way

the killer's does in *M*. It is surely a question of deliberate allusion on Reed's part. Later in *The Third Man* there are close-ups of a magnifying glass and fingerprints, as there are in *M*; an elderly balloon-seller appears in both films.

....

Holly and Anna get well ahead of their pursuers and take refuge in a cinema. (Anna has to pay again.) Holly sits behind her in the stalls and whispers to her to slip back to the theatre. 'What are you going to do?',

Anna asks as she makes to leave. Looking a little frightened, Holly says he doesn't know. 'Be sensible. Tell Major Calloway.'

Holly means to do just that and he rushes back to Sacher's to phone 'Callaghan'. When the concierge cannot give him the major's number, Holly asks instead for a car. He gets a broad smile. 'Of course, there's one waiting for you.' A heavy-set, slightly threatening man in a flat cap beckons Holly to follow him to a taxi parked outside.

As soon as he is sitting in the back, separated from the driver by a window and a metal grille, the car pulls out into the road and speeds along the cobbled streets, its brakes screeching. At first Holly is thrown back into his seat but he recovers himself and knocks hard against the window, calling out to the impassive driver: 'Have you got orders to *kill* me?' This is Holly the pulp writer again, getting carried away, but the frantic night drive through a city apparently deserted except for the watchful locals whose faces are cut into the sequence is filmed like a kidnap, shots of the hurtling taxi alternating with images of Holly trapped behind the grille, the driver indifferent to his panic.

Then they suddenly draw to a halt outside a building. The door opens and there is Crabbin. He brims over with welcoming talk. Since the guest of honour is late for the speaking engagement he had managed so completely to forget, Crabbin gets the introduction over in a flash: 'Ladies and gentlemen, I have much pleasure in introducing Mr Holly Martins from the other side.'

Holly's talk on the modern novel is a fiasco. As he mumbles answers to increasingly belligerent questions – 'Do you believe, Mr Martins, in the stream of consciousness?' – or just waits for the question to go away, Crabbin squirms, nibbling at his lower lip and dabbing his brow with a white handkerchief. Several disgruntled burghers give up and leave.

Well-dressed women are walking out as Popescu enters the hall. He spares Holly the embarrassment of trying to give an account of James Joyce by asking him whether he is working on a new book. Some fight and confidence return to Holly:

'Yes. It's called *The Third Man*.'

'A novel, Mr Martins?'

'It's a murder story. I've just started it. It's based on fact.'

Moments later the hall is all but empty and Crabbin, visibly relieved, brings the meeting to an official close, ready no doubt for a large drink with his mysterious companion. This is the last time the genial Wilfrid Hyde-White appears in *The Third Man*.

Two heavies in pale raincoats have joined Popescu. Holly eyes them suspiciously, the zither breezing up and down a scale, then dashes through a side door up a spiral staircase. The men follow him. At the top he finds another door and passes into a darkened room. The zither stops completely in favour of other sounds – a low squealing and a dry scratching. 'Who is it?' Holly whispers urgently. He turns on a light to see a cockatoo on a perch, bouncing up and down and squawking. As he climbs out of the window the bird perfectly aims a sharp peck at his hand and draws blood.

Troubled Viennese faces observe Holly's 'kidnap'; Holly is bemused then hunted

Popescu's men are close behind Holly as he slides down the rubble and casts long shadows on the walls of a narrow alleyway strewn with so much fallen masonry that it seems more like a tunnel. The sources of light are few and distant, so when he turns a corner into some sort of covered walkway he no longer casts a shadow but is silhouetted against a brightness at its end.

The zither has returned, stately but sinister. Holly clambers into the burnt and rusting wreck of a car. He manages to conceal himself and his pursuers move on past, allowing him to escape in a different direction and a safer one, cobbles under his feet not shattered brick and stone.

....

In an autobiographical foreword to the American edition of his book *Coca-Colonization: The Cultural Mission of the United States in Austria after the Second World War*, historian Reinhold Wagnleitner recalled Vienna in the 1950s:

> For us, the horrors of the Second World War were in the distant past, but still they were everywhere. Our everyday experience included quite a few mutilated men, and for the nicer ones we picked up cigarette butts from the streets. It seemed absolutely normal that most men and many women looked old and tired – and not only because we were children and they wore dark clothes. … Although most families with a Nazi past repressed and hid this past from the children, the war remained everywhere – and we did not need a war memorial to be reminded of the many ghosts roaming our streets.[45]

Maybe *The Third Man* is at its most intuitively political when it shows Viennese faces in close-up: vigilant, troubled, suspicious faces. At least one of them is a black marketeer, but who are the others? Perhaps one is Jewish, plagued by unbearable memories, another a paranoid bourgeois shamelessly suppressing a Nazi past, another an amputee in tattered clothing.

In *The Man Between*, Udo recalls his activities in World War II: the compromises, the lost ideals, the soul-death required to be an 'efficient unit of the military machine'. Hardly anyone speaks about the war in *The Third Man* but it is pervasive. The not-speaking matters. It involves, on the one hand, tact. A popular thriller is not yet the place for overt symbols, moral polemics or serious commemoration. But, on the other hand, there is no hiding from history, even or especially when it does not emerge into the open.

'What relevance has the rococo trifle in which Valli appears at the Josefstadt Theatre to the Viennese who come to it from the sort of ruins – and the sort of historical and social conditions – we see outside?'[46] There is no obvious relevance, because relevance would, for the moment at least, be too much. So the staging shows another world.

....

The film has reached a point where questions need to be answered. Did a third man tend to Harry's body after the accident? Who was the fourth man on the bridge? Who murdered the porter? How is the mysterious Harbin involved?

Though Holly is still jumping to glib novelistic conclusions, there is no disputing that he has rattled Popescu's cage. Those grey-coated henchmen definitely had violence in mind.

The dissolve is to Calloway a little while later, getting more irritated at Holly by the second: 'I told you to go away, Martins. This isn't Santa Fe, I'm not a sheriff and you aren't a cowboy. You've been blundering around with the worst bunch of racketeers in Vienna … and now you're wanted for murder. … What's the matter with your hand?'

'A parrot bit me.'

'Oh, stop behaving like a fool, Martins.'

Greene's writing here is beautifully crisp: the two men spar with one-liners. The uniformed Calloway paces around while Holly smokes, leaning against a pillar. The major tells the off-screen Paine to bring him the file on Harry and then sits down, ready to get serious.

The sergeant drags a table-mounted slide projector from the wall while Calloway pulls up a screen. When the lights go out, the first slide is a decorative painting of a rhinoceros, which Paine explains is something new for Mr Crabbin. It is replaced by a photograph of a young man apparently in

intense discussion with a soldier. It is Joseph Harbin. Calloway explains that Harbin, a medical orderly, acquired the supplies of penicillin that Harry and his accomplices then diluted, turning it into poison potent enough to kill patients or irreparably damage their minds. When Harbin was questioned he implicated Harry and Kurtz, but the investigating authorities wanted more evidence, which would expose the whole racket. Before they could get it Harbin disappeared. Holly gets the great line this time: 'This is more like a mortuary than a police headquarters.'

Another slide comes up on which Harry's right thumbprint is displayed next to the glass phial from which it was taken. A hypothesis of guilt is being substantiated. There follows a characteristically effective and economical montage of the authorities' forensic techniques and articles of evidence, accompanied not by Calloway's explanations but by the zither at its slowest, the strings audibly twanging and reverberating as they are forcefully plucked. A big close-up of Holly shows him concentrating but with his mind on other things too. The presentation has been successfully concluded.

On the way out Holly nearly bumps into Brodsky, who marches up to Calloway and demands Anna's fake papers. The Englishman starts to protest, his vestigial kindliness towards her showing once more: 'Oh – we're not going to pick her up for that are we?' The Russian shrugs him off and Calloway puts the passport on the desk. It is seen in close-up, a coda to the evidence montage, its serial number ('030.852') plainly legible, Anna's name handwritten at the bottom. There is a pitifulness about the shot, which comes from the juxtaposition of Anna's name – her life, her past – and the bureaucratic knowledge of it as a number and some paper to be passed between officials.

. . . .

Michael Ondaatje pauses during *In the Skin of a Lion* (1987) to reflect on the poignancy of silent film comedy:

> The tramp never changes the opinion of the policeman. The truncheon swings, the tramp scuttles through a corner window and disturbs the fat lady's ablutions. These comedies are nightmares. The audience emits horrified laughter as Chaplin, blindfolded, rollerskates near the edge of the unbalconied mezzanine. No one shouts to warn him.[47]

In the way he moves at the end of *Odd Man Out*, Shell (F. J. McCormick) recalls this poignancy. He scuttles forward like Chaplin's tramp. Two

Shell dances his way out of trouble in *Odd Man Out*

policemen pick him out with torches that illuminate like spotlights; he is a dancer on the pavement, scurrying along as if in a macabre premonition of *Singin' in the Rain* (Stanley Donen/Gene Kelly, 1951). He is diffident and afraid but he moves with a swagger. The exaggerated movement, like Chaplin's in *City Lights* (Charles Chaplin, 1931), makes up for a fear that there is no shelter in the city. The choreography of their bodies is careful and deliberate; there is a fugitive's alertness. Disaster could come at any moment, with no one there to shout a warning.

Cities are among the most fundamental of the cinema's subjects – cities not 'the city'. A city has many realities. The same street or building exists differently, depending on the point of view. It is not the same for the shopper, the lost child, the man on the run, the pickpocket, the immigrant, the policeman, the beggar, the tourist, the terrorist or the bomber pilot thousands of feet above.

Carol Reed was one of the great directors of city-experience, and what he emphasised was disorientation and alarm. His heroes are purposeful in the city but hunted. There are traps all about and an ambush is always expected. Often it comes, if the purposefulness is forgotten or made impossible by injury, delirium, grief or obsession. In film after film, characters stumble along a street, their minds disintegrating. It happens throughout *Odd Man Out*. In *The Fallen Idol* Felipe does the same, distraught, until a policeman stops him. *Outcast of the Islands* plays a variation on this, having Willems, consumed by lust to the point of derangement, paddle a canoe around the island village in search of Aissa (Kerima).

This frantic hurry is like a primal scene in Reed's work. It is counterpointed by a photographic trope – the image of a head held back

Johnny on the run in
Odd Man Out

Felipe on the run in
The Fallen Idol

Ivo and Susanne
(Claire Bloom) on the run
in *The Man Between*

against a wall, of a body wanting to disappear into shadow, of eyes sensitive to any peripheral movement.

The montage of evidence and surveillance explores, as very similar sequences in *M* and *Roma città aperta* (Roberto Rossellini, 1945) do, the affinity of bureaucracy and authoritarianism.[48] Calloway wields power over an urban environment – Vienna can be watched, staked out, mapped or photographed. But this power has a limitation. It freezes the city in a two-dimensional image or diagram – it is a stationary, fixed power. It does not entirely govern the fugitive's city, which is dynamically three-dimensional, in motion and topographic; so the fugitive has an advantage. He can move unpredictably, he can remain hidden, and he can move vertically as well as at ground level, on the look out for hiding-places and eyries above. *Odd Man Out*, *The Third Man* and *The Man Between* all insist on this advantage, showing their protagonists clambering up scaffolds, on window ledges, down winding stairs and mounds of debris – even moving and sheltering below ground, in the sewers. Or these running men take advantage of unsuspected vehicles (a hansom cab in *Odd Man Out*, the burnt-out car in *The Third Man*, a laundry truck in *The Man Between*).

But always their advantage is lost and they die, gunned down. There is great pathos in the fatalism of Reed's theme and the way it is worked out in the visual elaboration of space, height, distance and direction. Reed owed a debt to one film in this respect – Duvivier's *Pépé le Moko* (1937), which opens with a mock-documentary account of the casbah in Algiers where Pépé (Jean Gabin) hides out. It is a 'tangled labyrinth', a warren of cells, balconies, walkways and rooftops, with its own clandestine communication systems of knocks and warnings. Here Pépé can be free but he can never leave in safety. When he does, and is arrested, he commits suicide, disembowelling himself with a knife.

Forensic investigation in *M* and *Roma città aperta*

The fugitive's city in
Odd Man Out

The fugitive's city in *Pépé
le Moko*

Greene reviewed the film on its release, and he adored it, with its concern for 'the experience of exile common to everyone': 'I cannot recall [a film] which has succeeded so admirably in raising the thriller to the poetic level. ... The theme of no freedom anywhere is not lost in a happy ending.'[49]

The same can be said of Reed's poetic urban thrillers. The cities in them are also finally only prisons.

. . . .

At the Casanova, where a scantily-clad dancer is gyrating to bland jazz played by muted horns and a row of women sit at the bar ready to escort any interested male customer, Holly is getting drunk. He buys the club flower-seller's whole armful of blooms and, at the end of a long day, heads over to Anna's.

She is lying down and staring into space, the deep chiaroscuro emphasising her face and the monogrammed pyjamas she is wearing. 'HL', the initials read. There is a knock. She turns on the light and opens the door to Holly, bemused and amused at the same time. At first she is surprised and asks if the police are after him but then she realises that he has been drinking.

Holly is feeling sorry for himself. 'I'm going back home. … It's what you've always wanted, all of you.' He tries to play with the cat, dangling a piece of string from the bedpost, but it just yawns, jumps off the bed and up to the window sill, disappearing between two pot plants. (The windows are flung open, even though it must be cold outside in the Vienna night.) 'He only liked Harry,' Anna says without apology. Holly tries to avoid the question of whether he has seen Calloway, muttering nonsense about a parrot nipping a man, but Anna is grave and cuts through the small talk. 'He told you, didn't he?'

As Holly moves away from the sill, the camera (belatedly following the cat) zooms quickly towards it and the light foliage in the window box, then passes through it in order to have a view of the street below where a man, his face an indistinct white blank, is seen in long shot looking straight back.

This unexpectedly elaborate camera movement is like a division between acts. All of a sudden Holly and Anna are forgotten in a movement from inside to outside, from two-handed drama to a scene of stealthy observation. A star actor is waiting and watching in the wings.

As if alarmed by the camera, the man slips into the darkness of a doorway and there is a cut to a different shot, taken almost at street level, of the cobbles just below. The cat slouches round the corner, pads forward and mews contentedly as it nestles between a pair of handsome

Anna lost in thought and oblivious to Holly's advances

brogues, rubbing its cheek against their wearer's left leg. It plays with the shoelaces with relish.

Back inside, Anna is sitting sadly on the bed, the flowers cast to one side, her back to Holly. 'He's better dead,' she says, acknowledging that she never knew before quite how deeply Harry was involved in the racket. They are talking at cross-purposes. Anna is possessed by Harry: she can think of nothing else. But for Holly he is just an idea – the idea of a friend, a character in a bad novel about friendship. When he begins to complain about the fact that Harry must have assumed he would go along with the penicillin scam, Anna stops him short: 'Oh please, for heaven's sake stop making him in your image. Harry was real. He wasn't just your friend and my lover. He was Harry.'

. . . .

Welles was a nomad when he accepted the part of Harry Lime. He had left America in 1948, having finished shooting *Macbeth* for Republic. He hardly returned in ten years. Projects had fallen through, including versions of *War and Peace* and *Cyrano de Bergerac*, both proposed by Korda. (Though Selznick opposed his casting in *The Third Man*, he nonetheless had seen fit to hire Welles to speak the portentous voiceover for *Duel in the Sun*, directed by King Vidor and released in 1946.) Maybe Europe was a better bet.

He lived well on his travels but he was always short of money. When Reed approached him over a dinner in London about playing in *The Third Man*, his mind was on financing a film of *Othello* (*c*. 1603). He was offered, for a few days' work, $100,000, or twenty per cent of the film's profits. He opted for the cash – a disastrous decision that he always

Reed and Welles in the Vienna sewers

regretted. He signed on but then disappeared. Vincent and Michael Korda had to be sent to Italy to track him down, which they did with some difficulty, at which point they more or less forced him onto a plane.[50]

No matter that he had fun on *The Third Man*, not taking it too seriously, Harry Lime is one of Welles's great screen roles. It is astonishing the presence that Welles had from the beginning of his film career – that his larger-than-life, demagogic, mischievous, egotistical personality could so easily be authentic and hypnotic. From the start he seemed like an actor who was already distinguished, like a grand old man of the theatre or cinema, but he was twenty-six when he made *Citizen Kane* (1941).

Welles was always Welles and yet he was utterly compelling and convincing as Kane, Macbeth, Othello, Quinlan in *Touch of Evil* (Welles, 1958) or Falstaff in *Chimes at Midnight* (Welles, 1966). And Harry is another Kane, another Falstaff, a variation on squandered genius, infinitely alluring but discomfiting – overflowing with vital energy but, at some deeper level, falling apart, damned. There is no reason to doubt that someone like Harry could exist – on the make, adored, constantly spoken about, making up his own rules for his own purposes: Welles's own career proves it.

....

It looks like Holly is done with Vienna and Harry and Anna. Outside her apartment he strolls half-disconsolately, his hands deep in his pockets, kicking at a stray pebble. There is a cut to the doorway in a steeply tilted shot, the cat visible on its top step.

The zither plays high notes in simple figures until Holly is alerted by the cat's mew to a human presence in the doorway, at which point a short chord recurs. Holly presses up against a building and defends

Harry's inscrutable smile

himself with clichés spoken out loud: 'What kind of a spy do you think you are, satchel foot?'

It is very late. The streets are deserted but for the two men, though a tram and a car's horn can be heard some way off. 'Cat got your tongue? … Come out, come out, whoever you are. Step out into the light and let's have a look at you.' But Holly's shouting has woken a woman in an upstairs apartment and her disgruntled protests are heard as she turns on a lamp.

A wide beam of light cuts through the slight mist and illuminates the man in the doorway below. His hat, scarf and overcoat are all black so the moon of his face is disproportionately bright. His eyes fix first on the apartment window then they dart to Holly, who, in a reverse shot, looks back with astonishment. He is speechless.

There are three more cutaways from the man, and each time the camera returns to his face as it plays variations on a sardonic pout (though all the expression is in the eyes and the eyebrows). The hat is slightly askew and it emphasises the band of shadow that runs down the left side of his face, a stroke of black that seems to disconnect his large left ear. When the camera returns for the first time it zooms in so that this still face outlined by darkness with its quick, mobile eyes nearly fills the screen.

Holly finds his voice: 'Harry!' He starts across the road to the sound of the woman in her apartment finishing her tirade and closing the window so that the doorway is once more in impenetrable shadow.

. . . .

It is a great deal but it is only this: light falls upon a face. In the cinema the illuminated face can be a trope of salvation, as in the close-ups of Falconetti in *The Passion of Joan of Arc* (Carl Theodor Dreyer, 1927) – the light is divine.

In calling his novella '*The Third Man*', Greene was invoking Luke 24: 13–15: 'And, behold, two of them went that same day to a village called Emmaus, which was from Jerusalem about three score furlongs. / And they talked together of all these things which had happened. / And it came to pass, that, while they communed together and reasoned, Jesus himself drew near, and went with them.' Or Greene was invoking T. S. Eliot's version of Luke in part five of *The Waste Land* (1922):

Who is the third who walks always beside you?
When I count, there are only you and I together

But when I look ahead up the white road
There is always another one walking beside you[51]

So is there something of salvation here, in the reappearance of this man who has, in Greene's phrase, risen from the dead?

At the end of *Odd Man Out*, Johnny is near to death when he collapses in the garden of a terraced house. Snow has begun to fall. A curtain is drawn back in a window above him and the sudden light cascades onto his face as he lies spread-eagled on the cold ground. Given his earlier hallucinatory delirium during which the words of I Corinthians 13 ('when I became a man, I put away childish things') come to him, and given his halting progress on a 'white road' through the city towards 'crucifixion', it seems as if this shot may be part of a Christian allegory.[52]

Light falls on Johnny

The boys in the window see nothing of what happens below

But then there is a cut back to the source of the light, to the window out of which two boys look in delight at the descending snow – look up and away from Johnny, like the ploughman in Auden's 'Musée des Beaux Arts' (1938), with no clear sight of a fallen man and even less concern ('for him it was not an important failure').[53] There is no light from heaven and no 'dreadful martyrdom' here,[54] just an accidental light and the slow dying of a wounded man for whom few tears will be shed.

Christian symbolism is summoned up in *Odd Man Out* and then rejected. So, after all, Eliot's poem is more significant, with its sense of a world in which religion and ancient rites are a distant backdrop to modernised, mechanised and faithless urban life, with its cultural fragmentation and in all its profanity and banality:

Falling towers
Jerusalem Athens Alexandria
Vienna London
Unreal[55]

Thousands of years pass in these lines. Sodom and Gomorrah crumble in the desert heat, the great library at Alexandria perishes in fire, giving way as the ages rush by to a twentieth-century inferno – 'unreal' modern conurbations with their 'etherised', alienated populations, moving en masse over bridges, in mourning: 'so many, / I had not thought death had undone so many.'[56]

Eliot's liturgical cadences, and his litany of names, sound canonical. But the lack of punctuation reflects a loss of structuring values and traditions, an unmooring, a proximity to chaos in the years immediately after World War I. In this chaos old languages, like the ones Eliot samples throughout his poem, became redundant and hollow, and old habits of faith began to change. Greene and Reed were artists like early Eliot, for whom the sacred was powerful but not real, only remembered – or being forgotten.

The illuminated face can equally signal perdition. At the end of Welles's *Othello* (1952), in what may be a deliberate visual echo of Harry's appearance in *The Third Man*, Welles in medium close-up cranes up at the camera and the light source above it. In his magnificent delivery of Othello's parting words he has as little breath left in him as Mason's Johnny had. The great death-speech – 'I pray you ... Speak of me as I am' (V. ii) – is spoken in a suffocating murmur. His face swims in darkness. Chaos and black night are all around him, ready to swallow him, so far away is he from any god.

Othello: darkness closes in

There does not at first seem to be anything quasi-allegorical about Harry's unexpected illumination except in an allusive way – Reed cannot have forgotten the sequence in *Odd Man Out*, even if the staging of the scene in *The Third Man* had been exactly imagined in Greene's novella. The light from the window is rather a spotlight from the theatrical gods picking out a performer. Harry might begin to sing or to tap dance, grinning as he does so, in a bawdy music-hall routine.

But for all that, the shots of Welles are enduringly enigmatic and genuinely, powerfully iconic, as if they could be allegorical. What, anyway, is that expression on his unmade-up face? A smirk, a leer, a wistful grin, a bitter smile? It is a picture of confident self-possession – but is there anxiety and torment in it too? There could be nothing behind that look or there could be a lifetime's worth of disillusionment. What has Harry Lime lived through? Is he a devil or a cherub?

It is the cinema's equivalent of *La Gioconda* (*c*. 1503–7), Leonardo da Vinci's inscrutable vampire–madonna, who 'has been a diver in deep seas, and keeps their fallen day about her'.[57]

. . . .

Harry could not have made his getaway without being seen, though a cut to a view from down the street makes it credible. But, in any case, the dreamlikeness of the scene permits a vanishing act, as if when the spotlight went out a trapdoor allowed the magician to disappear. Distraction is easy here because attention is riveted to something else. Harry is not dead.

Holly reaches the doorway to find it empty even of the cat. Getting his bearings, he sees Harry's running shadow move against the wall of an alley, but when he follows, calling his friend's name and entering the square beyond, he finds nothing except a kiosk with faded posters pasted on it. Frustrated and confused, Holly bathes his face in a stone basin, then splashes the water against the sculpted putto alongside.

At the end of a dissolve Paine and Calloway are grumpily walking down the alley while Holly recounts the incident. 'This is where he vanished.' Calloway had thought Holly was out of his hair, but now that he is spinning stories again, the major is fed up. 'Yes, yes, yes, and then he vanished out there, I suppose with a puff of smoke and like a clap of—.' The zither interrupts his scorn as Calloway suddenly focuses. A point-of-view shot shows the shabby kiosk. The men stride over to it. Calloway opens it, looks at the steps inside and mutters to Paine: 'it wasn't the German gin.'

Down they go, Holly more puzzled than ever. Water pours down an underground weir and swirls in and out of the arterial channels and byways that lead off from a vast brick tunnel like a catacomb. 'It's the main sewer, runs right into the blue Danube,' says Paine – 'smells sweet doesn't it.' There is steel in the sergeant, underneath the yeoman's good cheer, and for the first time it shows. Looking into the mucky torrent, Calloway's head and shoulders fill the left of the frame as Paine, grim-faced, moves up behind him to hear his assessment. 'We should have dug deeper than a grave.'

It must be nearly morning, though it is still dark, when, by the light of flares, Calloway supervises the digging up of the coffin under Harry's headstone. Holly sits a little way off with a bottle of spirits, warming his glass with a flame. Filmed from an angle below ground level, the lid of the coffin swings open. Calloway and Paine peer down at the dead face, the major tipping his head slightly to get a clearer view. They are satisfied. 'Joseph Harbin,' Calloway tells an official, 'he used to work for Harry Lime.'

The graveyard dissolves into a rostrum shot of Anna's fake passport, open at the ID page. In her photo she wears a forced smile and looks dowdy and ten years older. The plot-trap has snapped shut and Anna's role is now indeterminate. She seemed so settled in her mourning that her reaction to the news about Harry is going to be interesting.

On the HQ first-floor landing, Brodsky hands the papers to the four-man patrol that featured in the opening montage. They take it with them up to Anna's apartment, her wrapped-up landlady badgering them vehemently as they climb the stairs. Anna is in bed but not asleep. A drying tear below her right eye catches the light. She is quietly afraid but resigned: she was expecting a visit from the International Police. The window is still wide open. When she walks out she gives the Russian soldier – the one who might represent her fate – a chilly look, stepping forward past the right edge of the frame.

Holly is waiting at HQ when she is marched up the stairs. 'I've just seen a dead man walking,' he manages to say before he is pushed away. Anna turns her head but pays no heed. Calloway is on the landing and he tells the patrol to bring her into his office for a minute. (Holly is told to wait outside.) The major is brusque: he wants to know when she last saw Harry now that Harbin's body has been found in his place. Something changes in Anna as she tries to take the news in without show. Caught between weeping and delight, her speech becomes a yearning whisper: 'Where's Harry? … I'm sorry I don't seem able to understand anything you say. … He's alive – now, this minute, he's doing something.'

Calloway wants to do a deal. Harry is in the Russian sector and if Anna will help in finding him Calloway will intervene with Brodsky. Anna responds with contempt: 'Martins always said you were a fool. … Poor Harry, I wish he was dead. He would be safe from all of you then.'

. . . .

Sigmund Freud, who fled Vienna in June 1938, bound for England, which he called 'a blessed, a happy land, inhabited by a kindly, hospitable people',[58] despised America. After a successful lecture tour in 1909 he declined all invitations to go back there.

The invitations were plentiful. In summer 1924, for instance, the Chicago publisher Robert McCormack sent a telegram offering him $25,000 to come and psychoanalyse the murderers Nathan Leopold and Richard Loeb, whose trial was a media sensation. A couple of months later the producer Sam Goldwyn upped the offer to $100,000 if Freud, as 'the greatest love specialist in the world', would advise on its on-screen depiction and perhaps even write a script. The *New York Times* reported the reply on 24 January 1925: 'FREUD REBUFFS GOLDWYN: Viennese Psychoanalyst is Not Interested in Motion Picture Offer.'[59] He set out his view of Americans in a letter to Ernest Jones on 12 April 1921: 'I think competition is much more pungent with them, not succeeding means civil death to every one, and they have no private resources apart from their professsion, no hobby, games, love or other interests of a cultured person. And success means money. Can an American live in opposition to the public opinion as we are prepared to do?'[60]

Then as now, such a view, however limited and unfair, was shared by many European artists and intellectuals, including Greene, who had 'the natural anti-Americanism of an upper-class Englishman' and was 'resentful of American assumptions of morality'.[61] The novella mentions in passing the 'Englishman who objects to Americans in general', and the sentiment also emerges in fiercer and uglier language. At one point Calloway muses that 'American chivalry is always, it seems to me, carefully canalized – one still awaits the American who will kiss a leper's sores'.[62]

Reed's views on the matter are less clear but there are hints that he thought along similar lines. In the BFI Special Collections there is a note written by him in which he planned to show 'a sign saying "American Information Office", which should look very pompous'.[63] In any case the hints were intelligible enough to Selznick. He wrote a strongly worded memo to Korda on 16 October 1948:

> THE SCRIPT IS WRITTEN AS THOUGH ENGLAND WERE THE SOLE OCCUPYING POWER OF VIENNA, WITH SOME RUSSIANS VAGUELY IN THE DISTANCE ... THE ONLY AMERICAN BEING AN OCCASIONAL SOLDIER WHO APPARENTLY IS MERELY PART OF THE BRITISH OCCUPYING FORCE ... I SPENT COUNTLESS HOURS GOING THROUGH WITH REED AND GREENE, AND GETTING AGREEMENT ON, THE TREATMENT OF THE WHOLE BACKGROUND OF VIENNA TODAY ... WE FRANKLY MADE THE RUSSIANS THE HEAVIES, IN PURSUIT OF THE GIRL. ALL OF THIS HAS BEEN ELIMINATED, EVEN WHAT WAS IN THE ORIGINAL SCRIPT. WE MUST INSIST UPON ITS RETURN, FOR PATRIOTIC REASONS ...[64]

Again no one seems to have paid Selznick any notice, except that the racketeer called Tyler in the script (Cooler in the novella) became Popescu: one American heavy was eliminated but no sympathetic American was added.

Holly is not some typical American, even if there is such a thing, but his character surely displays what Greene would have thought of as 'American assumptions of morality'. The Europeans in *The Third Man* have seen how war destroys morality; they have learned lessons about survival and pragmatism; they hide despair in cynicism. If they do not, like Anna, rebuff Holly completely, they at least snigger or frown at him, with all his breezy assertiveness and hasty judgments.

Holly is an innocent abroad, yes. He has some courage and vim in taking on Calloway. But he lacks any subtlety and he cannot see beneath the surface of people and situations: he does not understand complexity. So he thinks nothing of chasing after Anna, even though she is in mourning for his best friend. And he never registers his part in the porter's death. He is unable to work out the stakes involved because he never questions the accuracy of his moral compass. He lives in a world as limited as those of his trashy books – or of movies that must make a show of patriotism. He is a hypocrite because he effortlessly confuses principled behaviour and self-interest. He has no trouble smoothing out the awkward kinks in his restricted, self-justifying outlook on the world. He is at home with truisms and false modesty.[65]

No matter how likeable he might be or how basically well-intentioned, Holly Martins is dangerous because he thinks he has the makings of a hero, with God or virtue on his side.

. . . .

An eventful night has finally passed and, in the morning light, while workmen shovel behind him, Holly has managed to find his way to a distinguished-looking apartment block or hotel in the Russian sector. Winkel and Kurtz are standing on a neoclassical balcony like two gargoyles. They try to entice Holly up but he has only one thing on his mind: 'I want to talk to Harry ... Tell him I'll wait by that wheel there. Or do ghosts only rise by night, Dr Winkel?'

Harry's theme strikes up on the zither as Holly smokes by a carousel at the foot of the Prater wheel, which, against the low sun and streaks of cirrus cloud, towers above him into the sky. From this extreme low angle there is a cut to a shot of the deserted carousel, its wooden horses motionless. A figure appears in the distance, circling around before walking directly towards the embarkation platform. As Harry approaches he grins, his tongue jutting against his cheek. Still walking, he takes off a tan leather glove, Welles's baritone voice full of chuckles, as if this meeting were the easiest thing in the world and the most fun: 'Hello old man, how are you?' Holly returns the greeting but withholds his hand. Harry leads the way to the platform.

It is difficult to pinpoint the mood of this encounter between Holly and Harry. Neither of them is relaxed, of course, though Harry makes a good show of it with his grin and wisecracks and his amiable complaints about indigestion. (Maybe Harry learned from Popescu that speaking about dyspepsia can be a way of moving a conversation along, even if the

condition does, on reflection, imply self-indulgence and even bad
conscience.) There is intimacy between them but it is strained, and the
impression is that there is more to the tension than just Holly's
knowledge of Harry's murderous racket. While Harry mesmerises with
his quick talk, effortlessly switching between a threatening cynicism and
witty repartee, Holly is glum and glowering, a little priggish in his self-
righteousness. It is another sign that there is less to this great friendship
than meets the eye – that, at least, it had already gone stale some time ago.

The wheel fairly whizzes round, the view outside it back-projected,
as the two men tussle. Holly twigs that Harry informed on Anna to the
Russians and Harry does not deny it. Instead he half-heartedly offers
Holly a piece of the racket. Holly presses his advantage, asking him
straight if he has seen any of his victims. Harry is unmoved: 'Victims?
Don't be melodramatic.'

Harry slides the carriage door open and there is a view of the fair-
ground below, some people milling around in it, mere specks from that
height. 'Would you really feel any pity if one of those dots stopped moving
for ever? If I offered you £20,000 for every dot that stopped, would you
really, old man, tell me to keep my money? Or would you calculate how
many dots you could afford to spend – free of income tax, old man, free of
income tax.' Holly mutters that money will not be of much use to him in
jail. 'That jail's in another zone. There's no proof against me – besides
you.' Then Harry seems to threaten him, saying he has a gun and that 'I
don't think they'd look for a bullet wound after you hit that ground.' Is the
threat real? Perhaps, but Harry has too much charm for it to seem so.

Holly drops a bombshell when he reveals that the coffin has been
dug up. Just for a moment Harry is at a loss, but then he is back to his
cheerful self, dismissing any talk of harming his friend. Holly has sat
down, disgruntled.

An awkward encounter

'You used to believe in God,' he says.

'I still do believe in God, old man,' Harry replies, 'I believe in God and mercy and all that, but the dead are happier dead. They don't miss much here poor devils.'

Harry has been drawing a heart with an arrow through it in the condensation on the window, with 'ANNA' written above it – a little token of their relationship, like his monogram on the pyjamas she wears. The carriage has come back to ground now and, as Harry opens the door, he tells Holly to look after Anna if he manages to get her out of the mess she is in. 'Be kind to her – you'll find she's worth it.'

The emotions triggered by this momentous meeting, whatever they are, evaporate almost instantaneously as the two men step back onto the ground. Harry reiterates that Holly can come in on the black marketeering; he only needs to send a message to arrange a meeting – as long as he does not bring the police.

A great deal has been said, much of it very disturbing and rather confusing, though the writing has been so good that not all the implications are clear: Harry's rhetorical flourishes have sent up a smokescreen. The film could have been stopped in its tracks here if it had become didactic, expanding on Harry's morality, if it had tried to fix him as an outright villain.

Did Welles sense that? In any case the last words in the scene are simply outrageous comedy, concocted by Welles and left in by Reed, light relief, accentuated by the zither's return, to avoid any sermonising: 'In Italy for thirty years under the Borgias they had warfare, terror, murder, bloodshed – but they produced Michelangelo, Leonardo da Vinci and the Renaissance. In Switzerland they had brotherly love, they had five hundred years of democracy and peace, and what did that produce? The cuckoo clock. So long, Holly.'

. . . .

In *Citizen Kane*, Jedediah Leland, played by Cotten, lives for years in the shadow of his friend and employer, loved but always dominated by Welles's Kane. Parts of him – vital, inner parts – are eaten away because he cannot reconcile his devotion to Kane with knowledge of his tyranny and vainglory. Jedediah once lectures Kane about the desire for self-aggrandisement in his political ambition but he hardly gets anywhere and the next time he appears on screen he is drunk, asleep at his typewriter, part of the way through a devastating review of the opera debut of Kane's wife. After he comes to, he is sacked and he leaves the newspaper

Jedediah leaves Kane
forever …

… but, near to death,
cannot forget him

office with a look on his face that is grim, bitter and secretly satisfied.

There is an immediate dissolve to him years later, an ill old man answering a journalist's questions about the dead mogul. He says he never replied to a letter Kane sent him but still he chatters on, analysing and remembering his friend with a bouncy detachment that suggests someone who has been hurt and defeated enough to lose contact with intenser emotions. His last words in the film imply a death wish: 'You know that young doctor I was telling you about – well, he's got an idea he wants to keep me alive.' It is a horrible and heartbreaking picture of a love that has failed but remains compulsive and even fatal.

Jedediah's disastrous friendship, as well as the more successful one between the two actors, must reverberate in the scene in the carriage, though its echoes may engender some confusion too because Holly's love for Harry never seems convincing. Or if he has loved Harry, that love was waiting to show the resentfulness inside it. Even if a spectator is unfamiliar with *Citizen Kane*, he or she will detect something more in this scene than two actors exchanging lines – some charge of feeling and familiarity. For those who do know the earlier films, there is a reprise of the conundrum of defeat and ambivalence that Cotten had presented before. And this conundrum affects the perception of Harry because it is a reminder that it is going to be hard to judge him disinterestedly.

Welles always had beguiling personal charm. More than Kane, Harry is the character who personifies what is sometimes at stake in charm – what charm can excuse or disguise. It is important to state the facts of the matter. Audiences love Harry and they are right to do so, because this is fiction not a moral reckoning; film spectators know the difference. Fiction is a licence to suspend moral considerations. In drab Vienna, with its dour, afraid populace and oppressive military presence, Harry is a breath of fresh air. He is funny and warm when he talks and contorts his face. And there is Anna's devotion to him and his friends' loyalty, even though they are not the most salubrious of friends. To turn on Harry, then, when it comes to a moral reckoning, is to act like Holly, with righteous rationality and bad faith, and also to cut off much of the pleasure of *The Third Man* at its source.

But a moral reckoning must come in a critical study of the film. Harry is fascinating and enchanting. Is he also, though, a nihilistic psychopath? This is what David Thomson has repeatedly argued: 'Which of us wouldn't want to execute a real Lime? But movies teach us to enjoy wickedness.'[66] He continues: 'Lime is … proof of how the court of movie has let iniquitous monsters go free because of charm, smart lines, and knowing where the camera is.'[67]

And yet is there another kind of argument to make about Harry, even if it does not exonerate him? Say, for instance, that Harry has reached a point of extreme disillusionment, perhaps brought on by experiences during the war. What might he have seen? There would have been enough to witness to override faith and certainty. Maybe what he has in common with Anna is a loss of all belief; maybe, despite his ebullience and sparkle, the darkness of despair is on him. Maybe he has seen 'the horror … the horror', like Kurtz in Conrad's *Heart of Darkness* (1899). This is a hypothesis about his madness not an excuse for his actions – but the mad must always escape execution.

Welles cherished the idea of making a film of Conrad's story. (And did it hover in Greene's mind when he was writing the novella? There are enough structural and emblematic parallels.) In his biography Thomson, following James Naremore, quotes a speech Welles wrote for Kurtz:

> I'm a great Man, Marlow – really great. ... The meek – you and the rest of the millions – the poor in spirit, I hate you – but I know you for my betters – without knowing why you are except that yours is the Kingdom of Heaven, except that you shall inherit the earth. Don't mistake me, I haven't gone moral on my death bed. I'm above morality. No. I've climbed higher than other men and seen farther. I'm the first absolute dictator. The first complete success. I've known what many others try to get. ... I won the game, but the winner loses too. He's alone and he goes mad.[68]

Might Harry not have said something like that, perhaps if he had got a little further down the road of indifference and murder? Indeed is this not a version of his speech in the carriage, as he looks down on the 'dots' that are people and commends their deaths to Holly? There is, in any case, madness in that too.

And yet – and yet. Greene was clear about where Harry fitted into

the broader scheme of things when he had Calloway say in the novella that a 'racket works very like a totalitarian party'[69] – whose Führer, in this case, is Harry.

Remember the look in the porter's eyes – the scared surprise. He was looking at Harry, come to kill him by cutting his throat.

. . . .

Calloway is so close to Harry he is agitated. If only Harry can be lured into the open. But Holly demurs: 'Twenty years is a long time. Don't ask

The porter meets his nemesis

me to tie the rope.' As Calloway seems to give up, Brodsky walks in, smugly telling him that Anna has been identified as a Czech with no right to be in Vienna. The Russians will apply for her to be handed over at the next day's four-power meeting.

Holly's eyes fall on the passport. He walks to a window and looks out as Calloway says, 'I think this would have worked – with your help'. The camera fills in the gaps by moving from two mugshots of Harry in his police file on the desk to Anna's false papers next to it. Holly makes a decision: 'What price would you pay?' Howard's wonderfully controlled, expressive face hovers somewhere between a surprised smirk and a ruthless determination that permits of no surprise.

'Name it,' he says.

Accompanied by the sound of a train's shrill whistle, the image dissolves to a shot of Holly at the station, his arms hitched up on a fence, his head bowed as he waits for Anna. Paine escorts her to the train and sees her safely on board. She questions him about why they are doing this for her but makes no protest. She is content to leave Harry behind.

Holly's sentimentality has got the better of him and he saunters into the café on the platform, where Anna, who has made ready to leave, sees him. She had been so calm but now she is tense and, leaving behind her suitcase and a parcel, she climbs down and makes for the café.

The meeting Holly was imagining was never going to be anything like this. For just a moment Anna is free and open because she thinks Holly is booked on her train. But when he says he has come to see her off she knows immediately that something is wrong. 'Harry, what is it?' Holly is gentle; he seems to feel no remorse or doubt and takes no offence at being misnamed, though he corrects her. He tries to avoid any more questions by putting his coat round her shoulders, asking her to send a

'They have a name for faces like that'

wire when she gets out of the country safely and herding her back towards the platform. He just wants her to get away from danger in Vienna. But she struggles and resists, forcing her way back into the café as the questions burst out.

The dialogue becomes showy but both actors are marvellous. There is angry passion in Valli but Cotten suddenly looks old and lined. He is sheepish when he confesses that he is going to help Calloway take Harry. Then the zither returns, quiet and plaintive.

> ANNA: Poor Harry.
> HOLLY: Poor Harry – poor Harry. He didn't even lift a finger to help you.
> ANNA: Oh, you've got your precious honesty and don't want anything else.
> HOLLY: You still want him.
> ANNA: I don't want him any more. I don't want to see him, hear him, but he's still part of me, that's a fact. I couldn't do a thing to harm him. *The train leaves noisily.*
> HOLLY: Oh Anna, why do we always have to quarrel?
> ANNA: If you want to sell your services I'm not willing to be the price. [*She tears up her papers.*] I loved him, you loved him, what good have we done him? Love. Look at yourself. They have a name for faces like that.

She leaves without another word and Holly, bent over at the bar, cannot turn to look at her until she is out of the door.

What is the name for that face? Certainly it is hurt and dazed. But Anna meant something else: cowardly, feckless, insufferable. It is the face of someone who betrays.

The doors swing back and forth, then the camera tilts down to frame Holly's coat lying crumpled on the floor. Anna wants nothing of him near her.

. . . .

Sophocles' *Antigone* (c. 442 BC) was important to the European Left during and after World War II as a text about rebellion. Brecht revised Hölderlin's 1804 translation to make an explicitly antifascist version, set in 1945 Berlin, which he staged at Chur in Switzerland in 1948.[70] But before that, in February 1944, Jean Anouilh had presented an adaptation in occupied Paris.

Sophocles' protagonist, Oedipus' daughter, resists her uncle Creon, ruler of Thebes, when he insists that her brother Polynices, who has plotted his downfall, not be given a proper burial. She does so in the name of tradition and the gods: 'These laws – I was not about to break them, / not out of fear of some wounded man's pride, / and face the retribution of the gods.'[71]

But in Anouilh's version there is no such motivation. His Antigone makes no appeal to religious observance. She isolates herself completely, cutting any tie that may compromise her – refusing any entreaty, with an inviolable 'no'. 'I do not want to understand,' she says to Creon, 'I am here to say no to you, and to die.'[72]

The Nazi authorities did not seek to ban Anouilh's play even though it made a case for resistance. 'At the first performance the play was greeted with applause from both the French and Germans in the audience.'[73] Creon, in this version, is a tyrant who can lucidly defend totalitarianism in terms of the greater good or the need for order and stability, as the Nazis did.

Anouilh's brilliance was in showing how tyranny can be reasonable to such an extent that nothing is left in reason for someone who will not be subjugated. All that remains is brute, instinctive defiance anchored in personal principles that make no appeal to the commonwealths of reason, power or the state. Antigone will give no quarter to Creon and she responds with unpacifiable scorn when he speaks of her happiness:

> What will this happiness of mine be like? What kind of happy woman will little Antigone become? What small sins will she be obliged to commit, day after day, in order to get her teeth into a morsel of happiness? Speak up. To whom shall she have to lie, suck up and sell herself? Whom shall she let die as she turns away her eyes?[74]

Her speech is a form of suicidal despair. It would be denounced by Christian churches, rational or realist theories of ethics and liberal politics, but it is an unimpeachable form of protest for a time when, as Greene said, there is no freedom anywhere.

Anna is like Antigone – in spirit if not degree. Harry is her Polynices and she will never betray him. Time and again Holly and, to a lesser extent, Calloway make rational attempts to persuade her that Harry is a criminal and a killer, undeserving of her allegiance. Her definitive response is simply 'he was Harry'. Argument cannot sway her. Nor can Holly's dubious charms, which are especially ineffectual, and, for her, eventually, unpardonably corrupt because they are clothed in the devotion that she clings to at any cost. Her contempt for Holly is so profound because she had assumed that they shared a common concern.

Loyalty to Harry is all that matters to her. Loyalty and not love in the everyday sense.[75] She does not seek Harry out after Calloway confirms that he is alive. Their last meeting is accidental, in the café to which Holly has lured Harry. With a feral protectiveness that Harry understands immediately, barely registering her presence, the only words she speaks to him are words of warning.[76]

. . . .

Holly goes to Calloway to call the whole thing off: 'I want to get a plane out of here tonight.' The major and his sergeant look at him with hardly any surprise and no alarm, as though they had talked over this eventuality – and planned for it.

'She gave me these,' Holly says, and for the third time Anna's passport – it is the same one, the military police simply gave it back rather than issuing anything new for her trip – fills the screen. It is rent in two. 'A girl of spirit,' Calloway says with some admiration. 'It won't make any difference in the long run. I'll get him.'

'I won't have helped.'

'That'll be a fine boast to make.' It is a killer line spoken by a man of strong conviction to one who cannot understand conviction.

Calloway does not cajole or complain. He has something else in mind. On the way to the airport in a jeep, with Paine in the back, he asks Holly whether he minds if they stop. Calloway has an appointment. 'Why don't you come in too? You're a writer, it might interest you.'

Calloway makes his point

Three nuns with starched, steepled wimples are on duty in the silent children's hospital ward as Calloway leads Holly in to see the human cost of Harry's penicillin racket. The zither is appropriately subdued and mournful. The major whispers behind Holly's back as they look at a meningitis victim in a cot: 'Terrible pity, isn't it?' Holly takes in the view, which is never given to the audience, his face tight and sombre.

Paine is at the wheel after the visit is finished, leaving Calloway, who is as sure of himself as he could be, to sit like Iago at Holly's ear. Holly is hunched into his coat, shaken and pensive. Calloway makes wry small talk about the writer's life and manages to make it sound like an insult. He says Paine lent him *Oklahoma Kid* and in so doing gets another fantastic line: 'I never knew there were snake-charmers in Texas.' Holly seems to hear the note of scorn and he interrupts the chatter.

'You win ... I'll be your dumb decoy duck.'

....

Audiences loved Harry Lime for his suave wit, his cockiness, his unbending desire to live well and resourcefully. A legend had been born – and one that slipped out of the hands of its creators. First there was a series on American radio, performed, and occasionally written, by Welles. Many of the scripts (or, rather, short stories) for the series were published in 1952 by the British Sunday newspaper the *News of the World* in

a mass-market paperback volume.[77] They are flippant: full of capers, devious conmen, good-humoured policemen, femmes fatales and exotic locations – Algeciras, Athens, Becurata (in Saudi Arabia), Buenos Aires, Geneva, Hong Kong, Panama, Tangier. It is all very trifling, to be sure, but in recording there is always, of course, Welles's voice.

The transformation of Harry Lime into a globetrotting hustler and playboy was taken to even greater extremes in the TV series of *The Third Man*, pro-

Rennie (with Sheldon Allman) in 'Hollywood Incident', a 1959 episode of the TV series

duced for the BBC in twenty-one episodes broadcast between 1959 and 1964. Harry was played by Michael Rennie (Bradford-born but here speaking with an American accent). He is part private investigator, part multinational entrepreneur.

In a typical episode, 'Who Killed Harry Lime?' (1962),[78] a plane is bombed off Hawaii and the newspapers report that Harry is dead. The news threatens to destabilise stock exchanges around the world. But Harry is once again alive; dapper in a polka-dot dressing gown, he orders the news to be corrected before changing into a crisp white suit. The dead man is, in fact, Harry's business partner, Taggart. Harry's butler Bradford Webster, played by TV stalwart Jonathan Harris, intones some facts without a blush: 'Poor Mr Taggart. ... Nothing but one tragedy after another ever since we've been financing his enterprises. The Copa plantation fiasco, the Philippine gold-mining venture, the Sumatran fishery disaster.' Harry gets down to sleuthing and soon enough discovers that Taggart's wife was responsible for the bombing.

But the Harry Lime created by Reed, Greene and Welles has not been forgotten. Instead he has passed into the general culture, as indeed have the whole mood and look of *The Third Man*. Let a few examples suffice. In the promotional video for British New Wave band Ultravox's single 'Vienna' (Russell Mulcahy, 1981), the film's camerawork is cannibalised: running shadows flitter against walls, men in leather greatcoats stalk city streets at night. In Peter Jackson's *Heavenly Creatures* (1994), Juliet Hulme (Kate Winslet) fantasises about Harry. Much the most striking and direct cinematic tribute is to be found in Gus Van Sant's first feature, *Mala Noche* (1985), in which Harry's doorway appearance is wittily re-enacted shot for shot when Walt (Tim Streeter) encounters Johnny (Doug Cooeyate) in Portland, Oregon. More gratuitously, the controversial politician Peter Mandelson entitled his 2010 memoirs *The Third Man: Life at the Heart of New Labour*.

There have been reports of remakes. On 23 November 1989, the *Evening Standard* reported that producer Arthur Weingarten was intent on securing the rights as a preamble to a remake. On 14 December 1996, the *Sunday Times* stated that 'Oliver Stone will risk the fury of film purists next year by updating The Third Man to Modern Berlin'. Happily, nothing has materialised.

....

It is night in the Russian zone and the lights seem welcoming in the Café Marc Aurel. The zither music is like a sinister flamenco played on the guitar. Holly peers out of the window at the square beyond and, in a long panning shot, it seems deserted. Then a low-angle view shows a soldier in a greatcoat and a helmet perched next to a raised column and an impassive statue of an angel. Other soldiers wait with stern expressions on their faces. The close-up glimpses of silent human presences are intercut with images of empty alleyways. Calloway has set his trap.

The first soldier suddenly sees something: a huge shadow, two storeys high, of a human figure moving along the side of a building, a phantom on the wall. The camera returns to the soldier, then tilts down and zooms in to discover Paine, Calloway and another soldier hiding in a dark corner. As the person casting the shadow comes into view the tension goes out of the music and a waltzing theme is reprised. It is not Harry but an old man holding a large bunch of balloons.

As Paine and Calloway look on, Anna enters the café unannounced, her face full of reproach and anger. To the major's mortification the balloon-seller approaches. He sees them though they turn away as if to disappear. In close-up the man is aged and bald, with a copious beard and a twinkle in his eyes. His voice is a magnificent basso profundo. 'Mein

The ambush at the Café Marc Aurel

Herr, balloon? … Balloon, mein Herr?' Calloway tries to fob him off in German but it is Paine who gets the message across: 'Come on – *schnell, schnell* … Go on, scarper.'

Harry Lime's theme begins over a canted shot of a building whose roof has gone (though a couple of ornamental statues on the façade are still intact). In the background a tiny figure of a man steps forward high up in the shell of the building. Harry smokes as he looks down, like the lord of all he surveys. Another long panning shot moves through a quarter of a circle until the café is in view. The camera zooms in, then there is a cut to the interior.

Anna improbably tells Holly that Kurtz, who has now been arrested, told her where he would be. She says he is wasting his time: 'Harry won't come. He's not a fool.'

But Harry has come. He silently enters, framed once more by a doorway. Holly and Anna do not notice him at first and Harry hears the damning things Anna is saying. 'Honest, sensible, sober, harmless Holly Martins. "Holly" – what a silly name. You must be very proud to be a police informer.' Midway through her speech there is a cut to Harry, half-smiling. But when he hears 'informer' the expression changes, hardening into surprised anger. Did he really think Holly was going to come in on the racket? He draws a gun from inside his coat. Anna sees him and urges him to run for it, but Harry wants to get a shot at Holly and tells her to move aside, gesturing with his free hand. But before he can shoot, assuming that he would have done, Paine arrives at another door and Harry turns on his heels.

Paine raises the alarm and the square comes to life. The waiting soldiers spring forward to the sound of whistles and the barking of attack dogs. Harry scrambles down rubble, a fugitive in the city. Soldiers pursue him down a broken stair, but they are some way behind: Harry is seen in flight at the end of a narrow street. The wailing of a siren and the sound of a tram are in the air. The zither has ceased altogether.

Harry comes to a manhole and lifts its interlocking triangular covers. He descends into the sewers – followed by soldiers, with Paine, Calloway and Holly among them – running for his life.

. . . .

The penultimate scene of *The Third Man* is the 'purest' thing in the film, virtuoso in its execution. There is no music until the very end and almost no speech, but there is an abundance of sound and sensation that is, at times, almost abstract.

Holly is with Calloway and Paine, giving chase. As they pursue Harry there are shots of other military personnel, dressed in white jumpsuits, flocking into the sewers. There is nothing simply linear about the chase. Again everything is complicated by depth in space. In order to follow Harry the troops and law enforcers have to move vertically as well as horizontally, from walkway to ladder to tunnel. The sewers are not just a labyrinth, they are a hive.

The military police carry great torches. The beams of light striate the curved walls of the sewers' arterial tunnels, decorating them with shadows, or play on the surface of the rushing water, which glimmers back in the light.

Harry is seen in the emblematic shot of the fugitive man, his head and shoulders pressed against a wall. He sees soldiers rushing towards him, their torches glaring in the near distance. He ascends a spiral stair and then his upward-tilted face is in huge close-up, squinting against a light source: an escape route is already an entry point for his pursuers. As more reinforcements arrive, Harry runs on, bent over in a tunnel that can only be four feet high.

Dogs are arriving and some of the jumpsuited men are carrying flares, bringing another, flickering source of light to the underground chambers. The dogs bark, the men speak to one another and their boots clatter; water moves in a torrent or cascades down onto the stone floor below. The sound editing – or, better, the sound design – by Jack Drake is quite remarkable throughout. The different noises are distinct but they echo against one another, reverberating in the nooks and the lofty corridors below Vienna. There is a sort of hostile, barely intelligible cacophony. Harry again flattens himself against a wall as pursuers move forward from the place he was hoping to head to. He wants to be in the open air, not confined like this, but all light and sound are now a danger to him.

He pulls himself up metal rungs set into the wall, his face yearning still more intently for a way out, but again the manhole is being used by soldiers, so he must drop back down. Like a locust, a soldier emerges from a narrow tunnel. Harry's head can just be glimpsed looking out from above a weir. There is another montage of watchful faces and deserted passageways, a reminder that the city above ground was a confining place too.

Several soldiers stop and listen at one end of a wide brick tunnel. A knocking can be heard. They turn on a searchlight and pick out Harry fleeing in ankle-deep water. The next shot is from the other end of the tunnel, the light streaming down on Harry, who stretches his arms out as

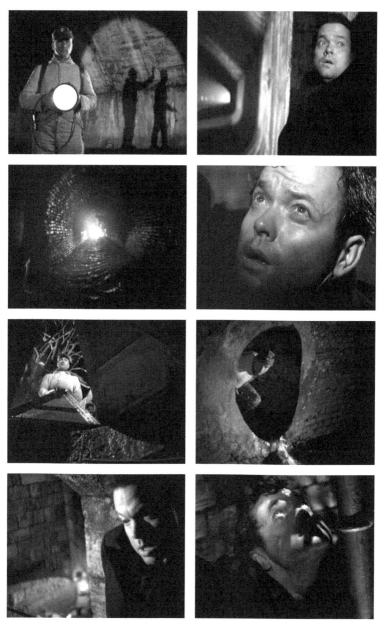

Harry at bay

if in crucifixion and as if to deflect the beams. There are whistles and shouts and the din of running boots.

More stairs, more inset rungs, another blocked escape route, another retreat. Certain rails and walkways seem familiar now: Harry is going in circles. He vaults a railing and carefully sidesteps along the precipice of a weir, moving faster as he gets across. But the soldiers are ever closer to him. Three of them use ropes to leap down the streaming bank and dive into a tunnel behind the curtain of water, appearing below the walkway Harry runs along.

He enters a large chamber in which voices congregate indefinably, their source and their distance from him impossible to make out. He can barely move, looking around, now this way, now that, a cornered creature with no idea where to run. He chooses an exit that leads to another bricked tunnel, and as he does so Holly sees him and calls his name. Harry ducks into an alcove, asking what Holly wants, trying to keep him from approaching or calling out. Harry has seen a wrought-iron staircase leading to the street.

Paine hears the talking and rushes forward, urging Holly to stay back. Harry aims and fires at the sergeant, who totters then falls forward

The criminal as tragic hero in *Pépé le Moko*

The criminal as tragic hero in *Odd Man Out*

to his knees, his expression pained and indignant. He dies with his face on the damp stone.

Harry makes a break for it and it gives Calloway the chance to hit him with a bullet. Holly and Calloway tend to Paine, for all that it is worth, while Harry, badly wounded, drags himself up the lower iron stairs. He is seen from the top of the staircase, sliding himself up, that face registering the first sensations of death but ardent still for some open ground. He fixes his eyes on a rusting grille above him.

Holly takes Paine's gun from his stiffening hand. Harry reaches the grille, grimacing. Viewed from street-level, his fingers clutch the grille. The scene has become powerfully, primally metaphorical. Iconography has superseded any morality: it is simply a matter of a yearning for freedom figured in the contact of a hand on metal bars – as at the end of both *Pépé le Moko* and *Odd Man Out*. The criminal at bay – trapped, injured, without any hope of escape – becomes a symbol of generalised existential tragedy, the symbol of 'no freedom any-where'. The wind blows in the night air as Harry's fingers reach up as best they may.

He is labouring for breath as he falls back to the top stair, unable to shift the metal obstacle. He gazes wearily at Holly, who approaches, not heeding Calloway's calls. The zither returns quietly, playing Harry's theme. The two men exchange looks. Harry is imploring and tears stand in his eyes. He glances down for a second. As Calloway rushes forward a shot rings out. Holly walks slowly back towards the major.

. . . .

The Third Man is not a coherent film – but this is one of its great strengths, rather than a shortcoming. The ending is a case in point. It was improvised late on in the shoot, with little planning. But Reed and Greene did talk it through:

> One of the few major disputes beween Carol Reed and myself concerned the ending, and he has been proved triumphantly right. I held the view that an entertainment of this kind was too light an affair to carry the weight of an unhappy ending. Reed on his side felt that my ending – indeterminate though it was, with no words spoken – would strike the audience, who had just seen Harry die, as unpleasantly cynical. I admit I was only half convinced; I was afraid few people would wait in their seats during the girl's long walk from the graveside and that they would leave the cinema under the impression that the ending was as conventional as mine and more drawn-out.[79]

This does not make complete sense. 'Unhappy' is not the same as 'unpleasantly cynical'; and how 'light' and 'conventional' is the film anyway, how much of an entertainment?

At the end of the novella Calloway watches Holly and Anna walk away side by side: 'before they turned out of my sight her hand was through his arm.'[80] Had Greene persuaded Reed to retain that ending for the film it would have been difficult to take. It would have undermined the severity of Anna's judgment of Holly, but under no circumstances could it have been construed as 'happy'. It would have been a bitter, empty culmination. What future together could reasonably be imagined for these two after what they have been through? It would have been a deeply unhappy happy ending. Better, then, that it ends as it does, bleakly but lightly, cynical about conventional forms of closure and the idea of a romantic couple.

Highly intelligent and superbly executed – but never disdainful of its audience – *The Third Man* is a hybrid work of art. Its mood changes from moment to moment. There are strong undercurrents of tone and emotion that pull it to and from despair or frivolity. It is also a film that insists on a variety of perspectives: it knows that there is no such thing as a comprehensive outlook on the world and that there is more which is secret and indefinable in people (and places) than is open and intelligible. It is this knowledge that makes it complex, shifting ... and classic. Because *The Third Man* does not cohere, it does not oversimplify its world and it does not demand to be understood in any single way.

It is for the best that it remains unclear whether Holly is an unforgivable hypocrite or a loyal friend with a good heart; whether Anna is a self-destructive obsessive or a woman prepared to sacrifice everything for the sake of dignity and principle; or whether Harry Lime is a lost soul, a malevolent sociopath or a charismatic martyr in a time without faith. Or all of these, or none.

. . . .

At the cemetery the priest speaks his benediction again over Harry's grave. Anna scatters some earth onto the coffin as Holly watches, his hat in his hand. His face is blank as his eyes follow her when she moves away. Behind him Calloway steps forward.

They get into a jeep together, both of them tired and pensive, both of them focused on Anna as she strides out ahead of them: 'I'll have to step on it if you're going to catch that plane.'

'Calloway, can't you do something about Anna?'

'I'll do what I can – if she'll let me.'

As they drive away from her Holly stops Calloway: 'One can't just – leave.'

'Be sensible, Martins.'

'I haven't got a sensible name, Calloway.'

Holly takes his case and walks slowly to lean against a cart filled with chopped wood parked by the side of the road. Anna is just visible, a small figure in the middle of the road.

That road winds across the Danube basin, northwestwards, through the cemetery into the old city of Vienna. It is flanked here by

Anna walks away

Holly is left alone

trees that are almost without leaves, though a few still flutter down. The zither-playing is careworn and slow. Calloway looks back, then drives away, leaving Holly to wait for Anna.

He has his hands in his pocket as he watches her once more, walking down the road at her own steady pace. She faces resolutely forward. As she draws level, I can still wonder if she will turn to Holly and say something to him. But she does not. She cannot spare even a glance. She moves on into an uncertain future, until she is beyond the camera's sight, beyond all sight.

Holly takes out a cigarette and strikes a match.[81] The screen begins to fade to black and – for an instant – only we notice how he seems, as in a mottled old photograph, to be etched forever into the image, with the light leaving it, a mere shadow of a man.

NOTES

· ·

1 All quotes from *The Third Man* have been transcribed directly from the DVD published in 2002 by Canal+ / Warner Home Video. The finished film often deviates significantly from the published shooting script (1968; London: Lorrimer, 1984).

2 For Selznick's contribution, see Charles Ramìrez Berg, '"The Third Man"'s Third Man: David O. Selznick's Contribution to "The Third Man"', *Library Chronicle of the University of Texas* no. 38, 1986, pp. 93–113.

3 Graham Greene, *'The Third Man' and 'The Fallen Idol'* (1950/1935; London: Vintage, 2001), p. 120.

4 Jonathan Rosenbaum, 'Welles in the Lime Light: The Third Man', www.chireader.com/movies/archives/1999/0799/07309.html, n.p.

5 Quoted in Charles Drazin, *In Search of The Third Man* (London: Methuen, 1999), p. 133.

6 Paul Tabori, *Alexander Korda* (London: Oldbourne, 1959), p. 13.

7 Graham Greene, *Ways of Escape* (London: Bodley Head, 1980), p. 122.

8 See Norman Sherry, *The Life of Graham Greene*, vol. 2 (London: Jonathan Cape, 1994), p. 242.

9 Tabori, *Alexander Korda*, p. 269.

10 See Charles Drazin, *Korda: Britain's Only Movie Mogul* (London: Sidgwick & Jackson, 2002), pp. 297–306.

11 See Drazin, *In Search of The Third Man* for an exhaustive, meticulously researched account of the making of the film (and much more besides).

12 George E. Berkley, *Vienna and Its Jews: The Tragedy of Success 1880s–1980s* (Cambridge, MA: Abt Books/Lanham, MD: Madison Books, 1988), ch. 24.

13 Audrey Kurth Cronin, *Great Power Politics & the Struggle over Austria, 1945–1955* (Ithaca, NY: Cornell University Press, 1986), p. 24.

14 Michael Korda, *Charmed Lives: A Family Romance* (Harmondsworth: Penguin, 1980), p. 230.

15 Quoted in Sherry, *The Life of Graham Greene*, p. 249.

16 Ibid., p. 253.

17 Greene, *Ways of Escape*, pp. 217, 219.

18 Quoted in James DeFelice, *Filmguide to 'Odd Man Out'* (Bloomington: Indiana University Press, 1975), p. 11.

19 James Mason, *Before I Forget* (London: Hamish Hamilton, 1981), p. 159.

20 Peter Ustinov, 'Extra Weight', *Sight and Sound*, December 1949, p. 14. Ustinov co-wrote (with Eric Ambler) *The Way Ahead*. See also Welles's remark in a 1982 TV interview that Reed 'was the real actors' director. His joy was in your work, not in seeing something of his come to life. He as exceptional in that case.' Transcribed in Mark W. Estrin (ed.), *Orson Welles: Interviews* (Jackson: University Press of Mississippi, 2002), p. 204.

21 Quoted in Michael Munn, *Trevor Howard: The Man and His Films* (London: Robson Books, 1989), p. 39.

22 Greene, *Ways of Escape*, p. 124. Some years later a newspaper interviewer recorded Cotten's memory of the name-change: 'He complained to Graham Greene that Rollo was a sissy name in America. Greene changed it to Holly Martins. "After that I stopped complaining for fear he'd change it to Pansy"' (John Crosby, 'The Second Man', *Observer*, 6 January 1969).

23 Michael Shelden, *Graham Greene: The Man Within* (London: William Heinemann, 1994), p. 322.

24 Quoted in David Parkinson (ed.), *The Graham Greene Film Reader: Mornings in the Dark* (Manchester: Carcanet, 1993), p. 557 (interview by Quentin Falk, National Film Theatre, 3 September 1984).

25 Quoted in Berg, '"The Third Man"'s Third Man', p. 103.

26 'THE THIRD MAN Conference Notes 8/17/48', Third Man Scripts, Carol Reed Collection, BFI Special Collections. Unless otherwise specified, all archival material referred to hereafter is to be found in these boxes.

27 Draft Script, p. 43 (scene 25).

28 Draft Script, pp. 19–20 (scene 13). The typescript of the short story is dated 'March 2–April 24, 1948', the last version of the script (from which Carter has disappeared and in which Kurtz's phone call is taken in the lobby at Sacher's) 20 September 1948. The 'Treatment', which presumably predates the draft script, has Holly take Kurtz's call while lying awake and fully clothed on his hotel bed. The embellishment of the scene in the draft script seems all the more unnecessary given that it apparently supplants a more economical version of it.

29 See microfiches for *The Third Man*, BFI National Library, as well as Carol Reed's clippings books, Carol Reed Collection, BFI Special Collections.

30 See some characteristically acute remarks about the film's style by James Naremore, *More Than Night: Film Noir in Its Context* (Berkeley: University of California Press, 1998), p. 79: 'on the one hand, the emotional flourishes and intensities of melodrama are treated with modernist skepticism; but, on the other hand, scenes of everyday life are haunted by a bloody and romantic passion.'

31 For succinct biographies and an account of the two actors' time under contract to Selznick, see Ronald Bowers, *The Selznick Players* (South Brunswick, NJ: A. S. Barnes, 1976).

32 S. S. Prawer, letter to the author, 13 September 2002.

33 Ibid.

34 Korda, *Charmed Lives*, pp. 229–30.

35 Manny Farber, review, *Nation* vol. 170 no. 13, 1 April 1950, p. 307.

36 Raymond Durgnat, *Films and Feelings* (London: Faber & Faber, 1967), p. 31.

37 For a fuller account of Karas's participation and his later fortunes, see Drazin, *In Search of The Third Man*, ch. 8.

38 Parkinson (ed.), *The Graham Greene Film Reader*, p. 243 (*Night and Day*, 9 December 1937).

39 Terence Pettigrew, *Trevor Howard: A Personal Biography* (London: Peter Owen, 2001), p. 94.

40 Rosenbaum, 'Welles in the Lime Light', n.p.

41 Duncan Petrie, *The British Cinematographer* (London: BFI, 1996), p. 117.

42 Greene, 'The Third Man', p. 66.

43 Graham Greene, *The Power and the Glory* (1940; London: Vintage, 2001), pp. 67, 68.

44 Graham Greene, *The Quiet American* (1955; Harmondsworth: Penguin, 1962), p. 162.

45 Reinhold Wagnleitner, *Coca-Colonization: The Cultural Mission of the United States in Austria after the Second World War*, trans. by Diana M. Wolf (1991; Chapel Hill: University of North Carolina Press, 1994), p. ix.

46 S. S. Prawer, letter to the author, 11 September 2002.

47 Michael Ondaatje, *In the Skin of a Lion* (1987; Toronto: Vintage, 1996), p. 43.

48 See Anton Kaes, *M* (London: BFI Film Classics, 1999), ch. 3; David Forgacs, *Rome Open City* (London: BFI Film Classics, 2000), pp. 34–45.

49 Parkinson (ed.), *The Graham Greene Film Reader*, pp. 193, 194 (*Spectator*, 23 April 1937).

50 See Korda, *Charmed Lives*, pp. 223–5; Barbara Leaming, *Orson Welles: A Biography* (New York: Viking, 1985), pp. 362–3.

51 T. S. Eliot, *The Complete Poems and Plays* (London: Faber & Faber, 1969), p. 73.

52 See Dai Vaughan, *Odd Man Out* (London: BFI Film Classics, 1995), pp. 65–9.

53 W. H. Auden, *Collected Poems*, ed. Edward Mendelson (1976; London: Faber & Faber, 1991), p. 179.

54 Ibid.

55 Eliot, *Complete Poems*, p. 73.

56 Ibid., p. 62.

57 Walter Pater, *The Renaissance* (1873; Oxford: Oxford University Press, 1986), p. 80.

58 Quoted in Peter Gay, *Freud: A Life for Our Time* (1988; London: J. M. Dent & Sons, 1989), p. 631.

59 Ibid., p. 454.

60 R. Andrew Paskauskas (ed.), *The Complete Correspondence of Sigmund Freud and Ernest Jones 1908–1939* (Cambridge, MA: Belknap Press of Harvard University Press, 1993), p. 419.

61 Michael Korda, 'The Third Man', *New Yorker* vol. 72 no. 5, 25 March 1996, p. 45.

62 Greene, 'The Third Man', pp. 56, 94.

63 '"THE THIRD MAN" – Notes C.R.', 21 May 1948.

64 Rudy Behlmer (ed.), *Memo from David O. Selznick* (New York: Viking Press, 1972), p. 386.

65 Raymond Durgnat, in 'Some Lines of Inquiry into Post-war British Crimes', in Robert Murphy (ed.), *The British Cinema Book*, 2nd edn (1997; London: BFI, 2001), p. 144, calls Holly '*culpably* innocent'. See also Andrew Sarris, 'The Stylist Goes to Hollywood: An Analysis of Carol Reed's Work for the Cinema (Part II)', *Films and Filming*, October 1957, p. 12: 'With Lime's death, Martins finds himself in an emotional wasteland created by his inability to feel any guilt … Martins, Lime and Calloway represent three approaches to the problem of evil. Martins externalises it in comfortable platitudes. Lime identifies with evil in a manner that is partly heroic and partly narcissistic. Calloway attacks evil in terms of bureaucratic disorder.' Robert F. Moss, *The Films of Carol Reed* (Basingstoke: Macmillan, 1987), p. 181: 'Martins operates by a standardized morality that is simply too one-eyed for the layered intricacies of real life – especially in the confusing netherworld of Vienna.'

66 David Thomson, *Rosebud: The Story of Orson Welles*, p. 295.

67 David Thomson, 'Reeds and Trees', *Film Comment* vol. 30 no. 4, July–August, 1994, p. 22.

68 Quoted in Thomson, *Rosebud*, p. 289, from James Naremore, *The Magic World of Orson Welles*, 2nd edn (1978; Dallas, TX: Southern Methodist University Press, 1989), p. 144. See also Naremore's remark in *More Than Night*, p. 75, that Holly 'resembles both a Jamesian innocent and a Conradian secret sharer. Like Marlow in *Heart of Darkness*, Martins is an impetuous, sentimental romantic; also like Marlow, he searches out a villain who makes a delayed entrance.'

69 Greene, *'The Third Man'*, p. 80.

70 See Bernard Knox's introduction to *Antigone* in Sophocles, *The Three Theban Plays*, trans. by Robert Fagles (London: Penguin Classics, 1984), p. 36. Marc Ferro calls Anna 'a modern Antigone' in *Cinema and History*, trans. by Naomi Greene (1977; Detroit, MI: Wayne State University Press, 1988), p. 127.

71 Sophocles, *The Three Theban Plays*, p. 82.

72 Jean Anouilh, *Antigone* (1944; Paris: La Table Ronde, 1975), p. 88. Translations from the French are by the present author.

73 Knox, 'Introduction', p. 36.

74 Anouilh, *Antigone*, p. 99.

75 See an unsigned document, 'ANNA: Story Thread': 'She will do nothing to harm Lime. Lime is still Lime, but Anna has changed … she doesn't want him any more but he's "in her". No blame for Lime, no hurt over his callousness as regards her.'

76 Korda signed a contract with Anouilh on 20 February 1947. The playwright was paid 700,000 francs to adapt *Anna Karenina* (plus £1,000 for the French-language copyright), which Julien Duvivier filmed later that year. The contract is Item a/018(i), box 2, London Film Productions Collection, BFI Special Collections.

77 Orson Welles et al., *The Lives of Harry Lime* (London: News of the World Pocket Book, 1952).

78 A 16mm viewing copy of this episode is held in the National Film and Television Archive.

79 Greene, *Ways of Escape*, p. 125. The shooting of the ending is described by Cotten in his autobiography, *Vanity Will Get You Somewhere* (London: Columbus, 1987), p. 98.

80 Greene, *'The Third Man'*, p. 119.

81 Nicholas Christopher gives a compelling account of the ending of the US version of the film in *Somewhere in the Night: Film Noir and the American City* (New York: Free Press, 1997), p. 75: 'the film fades – not to black, but to white. A fade to white. Blank as the sterile road that stretches out before Martins, who has become the ghost of himself and of Lime. A peculiarly American ghost, embodying the pale remains of both their thwarted ambitions.'

CREDITS

· ·

The Third Man

United Kingdom/USA
1949

Directed by
Carol Reed
Produced by
Carol Reed
Screen Play by
Graham Greene
Original Story by
Graham Greene
Photographed by
Robert Krasker
Editor
Oswald Hafenrichter
Sets Designed by
Vincent Korda
with
John Hawkesworth
Joseph Bato
Zither Music Played by
Anton Karas

©London Film Productions
Ltd.
Production Companies
A London Film production
Presented by Alexander
Korda, David O. Selznick
Carol Reed's production
Associate Producer
Hugh Perceval
In Charge of B Unit
George Pollock
**B Unit
Accountant/Cashier**
R. Reader
Production Manager
T.S. Lyndon-Haynes
Production Secretary
Teresa Deans
**B Unit Production
Assistant**
Robert Dunbar

Assistant Director
Guy Hamilton
2nd Assistant Director
Jack Causey
3rd Assistant Director
Jack Green
Continuity
Peggy McClafferty
Assistant Continuity
Angela Allen
Additional Photography
John Wilcox
Stan Pavey
Hans Schneeberger
Camera Operators
E. Scaife
Denys Coop
B Unit Camera Operator
Monty Berman
Focus Puller
Geoffrey P. Meldrum
B Unit Focus Puller
John von Kotze
Clapper Loader
Alan McCabe
Loader
J. Bicknell
Camera Grip
Joe Vincent
Chief Floor Electrician
H. Mackay
Electricians
Bert Whitear
S. Dye
Archie Dansie
Stills
Len Lee
Assembly Cutter
Peter Taylor
Assistant Editor
Derek Armstrong
Assistant Cutters
Ken Behrens
David Eady
Extra Assistant Cutter
Michael Coton

Assistant Art Directors
Ferdinand Bellan
James Sawyer
Set Dresser
Dario Simoni
Production Buyer
George Durant
Chief Floor Props
Sydney Leggett
Floor Props
Bobby Murrell
J. Larkin
F. Dann
Standby Carpenter
W. Nichols
Standby Painter
P. Tindle
Standby Plasterer
E. Greenleaf
Standby Rigger
J. Culley
Stagehands
A. Southall
H. Turner
Wardrobe
Ivy Baker
Wardrobe Master
George Murray
**Ladies' Assistant
Wardrobe**
Gene Hornsby
**Men's Assistant
Wardrobe**
Dickie Richardson
Make-up
George Frost
Assistant Make-up
Peter Evans
Hairdressing
J. Shear

Assistant Hairdresser
Iris Tilley
Sound Supervisor
John Cox
Sound Recording
Bert Ross
Red Law
B Unit Sound Recordist
George Adams
Sound Camera Operator
James Dooley
B Unit Sound Camera Operator/Maintenance
P. Jackson
Boom Operator
Jack Davies
Sound Maintenance
Dick Longstaff
Sound Editor
Jack Drake
Austrian Adviser
Elizabeth Montagu
Publicity
Enid Jones
Prologue Narrator
Carol Reed
US Version Prologue Narrator
Joseph Cotten

Cast
Joseph Cotten
Holly Martins
Valli
Anna Schmidt
Orson Welles
Harry Lime
Trevor Howard
Major Calloway
Paul Hoerbiger
Karl, Harry's porter
Ernst Deutsch
'Baron' Kurtz

Erich Ponto
Dr Winkel
Siegfried Breuer
Popescu
Hedwig Bleibtreu
Anna's landlady
Bernard Lee
Sergeant Paine
Wilfrid Hyde-White
Crabbin
[uncredited]
Reed De Rouen
American MP at railway station
Eric Pohlmann
Smolka bartender
Paul Hardtmuth
Hartman, hall porter at Sacher's
Annie Rosar
Karl's wife
Herbert Halbik
Hansl
Jenny Werner
Hilde, Winkel's maid
Alexis Chesnakov
Colonel Brodsky
Frederick Schrecker
Hansl's father
Thomas Gallagher
taxi driver
Martin Boddey
Russian military police
Geoffrey Keen
British military police
Lily Kahn
nurse
Leo Bieber
barman at Casanova Club
Nelly Arno
Kurtz's mother
Anthony Higginson
page
Geoffrey Wade
underporter
Walter Hortner
barman at Sacher's

Martin Miller
head waiter
Rona Grahame
Holga Walrow
Josefstadt Theatre people
Harry Belcher
Michael Connor
men chasing Holly
Jack Arrow
Reg Morris
Stephen Gray
Duncan Ryder
international patrol A
Brooks Kyle
Ray Browne
Arthur Hall
Howard Leighton
international patrol B
Gordon Tanner
Michael Godfrey
Guy de Monceau
Arthur Barrett
international patrol C
Paul Carpenter
Vernon Greeves
international patrol D
Hugo Schuster
waiter
Charles Irwin
Colonel O'Sullivan
Peter Fontaine

9360 feet
104 minutes 1 second
Black and White

Interiors filmed at
Shepperton Studios

Credits compiled by
Markku Salmi,
BFI Filmographic Unit

SELECT BIBLIOGRAPHY

Berg, Charles Ramìrez, '"The Third Man"'s Third Man: David O. Selznick's Contribution to "The Third Man",' *Library Chronicle of the University of Texas* no. 38, 1986, pp. 93–113.

Bowers, Ronald, *The Selznick Players* (South Brunswick, NJ: A. S. Barnes, 1976).

Christopher, Nicholas, *Somewhere in the Night: Film Noir and the American City* (New York: The Free Press, 1997).

Ciompi, Valeria and Miguel Marías (eds), *Carol Reed* (San Sebastián: Festival Internacional de Cine de San Sebastián / Filmoteca Española, 2000).

Cotten, Joseph, *Vanity Will Get You Somewhere* (London: Columbus, 1987).

DeFelice, James, *Filmguide to 'Odd Man Out'* (Bloomington: Indiana University Press, 1975).

Drazin, Charles, *In Search of The Third Man* (London: Methuen, 1999).

——, *Korda: Britain's Only Movie Mogul* (London: Sidgwick & Jackson, 2002).

Driver, Paul, 'A Third Man Cento', *Sight and Sound* vol. 59 no. 1, Winter 1989–90, pp. 36–41.

Durgnat, Raymond, 'Some Lines of Inquiry into Post-war British Crime', in Robert Murphy (ed.), *The British Cinema Book*, 2nd edn (1997; London: BFI, 2001), pp. 135–45.

Greene, Graham, *'The Third Man' and 'The Fallen Idol'* (1950 / 1935; London: Vintage, 2001).

——, *The Third Man* (1968; London: Lorrimer, 1984).

——, *Ways of Escape* (London: The Bodley Head, 1980).

——, *The Graham Greene Film Reader: Mornings in the Dark*, ed. by David Parkinson (Manchester: Carcanet, 1993).

Falk, Quentin, *Travels in Greeneland: The Complete Guide to the Cinema of Graham Greene*, 3rd edn (1984; Richmond, Surrey: Reynolds & Hearn, 2000).

Farber, Manny, review, *Nation* vol. 170 no. 13, 1 April 1950, pp. 306–7.

Hoare, John, *The Third Man* (London York Press / York Film Notes, 2000).

Knight, Vivienne, *Trevor Howard: A Gentleman and A Player* (London: Muller, Blond & White, 1986).

Korda, Michael, *Charmed Lives: A Family Romance* (1979; Harmondsworth, Middlesex: Penguin, 1980).

——, 'The Third Man', *New Yorker* vol. 72 no. 5, 25 March 1996, pp. 45–51.

Kulik, Karol, *Alexander Korda: The Man Who Could Work Miracles* (London: W. H. Allen, 1975).

Leaming, Barbara, *Orson Welles: A Biography* (New York: Viking, 1985).

Moss, Robert F., *The Films of Carol Reed* (Basingstoke, Hampshire: Macmillan, 1987).

Munn, Michael, *Trevor Howard: The Man and His Films* (London: Robson Books, 1989).

Naremore, James, *The Magic World of Orson Welles*, 2nd edn (1978; Dallas, TX: Southern Methodist University Press, 1989).

——, *More Than Night: Film Noir and Its Contexts* (Berkeley: University of California Press, 1998).

Pettigrew, Terence, *Trevor Howard: A Personal Biography* (London: Peter Owen, 2001).

Rosenbaum, Jonathan, 'Welles in the Lime Light: The Third Man', www.chireader.com/movies/archives/1999/0799/07309.html.

Sarris, Andrew, 'First of the Realists: An Analysis of Carol Reed's Work for the Cinema', *Films and Filming*, September 1957, pp. 9–10, 32.

——, 'The Stylist Goes to Hollywood: An Analysis of Carol Reed's Work for the Cinema (Part II)', *Films and Filming*, October 1957, pp. 11–12, 30.

Memo from David O. Selznick, ed. by Rudy Behlmer (New York: Viking Press, 1972).

Shelden, Michael, *Graham Greene: The Man Within* (London: William Heinemann, 1994).

Sherry, Norman, *The Life of Graham Greene*, 2 vols (London: Jonathan Cape, 1989 / 1994).

Tabori, Paul, *Alexander Korda* (London: Oldbourne, 1959).

Thomson, David, 'Greene in the Dark', *Film Comment* vol. 27 no. 4, July–August 1991, pp. 18–25.

——, *Showman: The Life of David O. Selznick* (New York: Alfred A. Knopf, 1992).

——, 'Reeds and Trees', *Film Comment* vol. 30 no. 4, July–August 1994, pp. 14–23.

——, *Rosebud: The Story of Orson Welles* (New York: Alfred A. Knopf, 1996).

Timmermann, Brigitte and Frederick Baker, *Der Dritte Mann: Auf den Spuren eines Filmklassikers* (Vienna: Czernin Verlag, 2002).

Vaughan, Dai, *Odd Man Out* (London: BFI Film Classics, 1985).

Wapshott, Nicholas, *The Man Between: A Biography of Carol Reed* (London: Chatto & Windus, 1990).

Welles, Orson, Sigmund Miller, Robert Cenedella, Joseph Cochran, Carl Jampel, Jonquil Anthony, Virginia Cooke, Peter Lyon, Bud Lesser and Irvan Ashkinazy, *The Lives of Harry Lime* (London: News of the World Pocket Book, 1952).

Orson Welles: Interviews, ed. by Mark W. Estrin (Jackson: University Press of Mississippi, 2002).

Wollen, Peter, 'The Vienna Project', *Sight and Sound* vol. 9 no. 7 (NS), July 1999, pp. 16–19.

ALSO PUBLISHED

An Actor's Revenge
Ian Breakwell

L'Âge d'or
Paul Hammond

L'Année dernière à Marienbad
Jean-Louis Leutrat

Annie Hall
Peter Cowie

L'Atalante
Marina Warner

L'avventura
Geoffrey Nowell-Smith

Belle de Jour
Michael Wood

The Big Heat
Colin McArthur

The Big Sleep
David Thomson

The Birds
Camille Paglia

Blackmail
Tom Ryall

The Blue Angel
S. S. Prawer

Bonnie and Clyde
Lester D. Friedman

Boudu Saved from Drowning
Richard Boston

Bride of Frankenstein
Alberto Manguel

Brief Encounter
Richard Dyer

Das Cabinet des Dr. Caligari
David Robinson

Cat People
Kim Newman

Chinatown
Michael Eaton

Citizen Kane
Laura Mulvey

Double Indemnity
Richard Schickel

Les Enfants du paradis
Jill Forbes

42nd Street
J. Hoberman

"Fires Were Started – "
Brian Winston

The Ghost and Mrs Muir
Frieda Grafe

Greed
Jonathan Rosenbaum

Gun Crazy
Jim Kitses

High Noon
Phillip Drummond

I Know Where I'm Going!
Pam Cook

In a Lonely Place
Dana Polan

It's a Gift
Simon Louvish

Ivan the Terrible
Yuri Tsivian

Kind Hearts and Coronets
Michael Newton

The Life and Death of Colonel Blimp
A. L. Kennedy

Lolita
Richard Corliss

M
Anton Kaes

The Magnificent Ambersons
V. F. Perkins

The Manchurian Candidate
Greil Marcus

A Matter of Life and Death
Ian Christie

Meet Me in St. Louis
Gerald Kaufman

Metropolis
Thomas Elsaesser

Mother India
Gayatri Chatterjee

Napoléon
Nelly Kaplan

The Night of the Hunter
Simon Callow

La Nuit américaine
Roger Crittenden

October
Richard Taylor

Odd Man Out
Dai Vaughan

Olympia
Taylor Downing

Palm Beach Story
John Pym

Pépé le Moko
Ginette Vincendeau

Performance
Colin MacCabe

Queen Christina
Marcia Landy & Amy Villarejo

Red River
Suzanne Liandrat-Guigues

Rio Bravo
Robin Wood

Rocco and his Brothers
Sam Rohdie

Rome Open City
David Forgacs

Sanshô Dayû
Dudley Andrew & Carole Cavanaugh

The Searchers
Edward Buscombe

Seven Samurai
Joan Mellen

The Seventh Seal
Melvyn Bragg

Shadows
Ray Carney

Shane
Edward Countryman & Evonne von Heussen-Countryman

Singin' in the Rain
Peter Wollen

Stagecoach
Edward Buscombe

Sunrise – A Song of Two Humans
Lucy Fischer

Taxi Driver
Amy Taubin

Things to Come
Christopher Frayling

To Be or Not to Be
Peter Barnes

Vertigo
Charles Barr

Went the Day Well?
Penelope Houston

Wild Strawberries
Philip & Kersti French

The Wizard of Oz
Salman Rushdie